BRING IT ON

DHIREN HARCHANDANI

PASSIONPRENEUR®
PUBLISHING

BRING IT ON

How to Master Your Inner Game

DHIREN HARCHANDANI

PASSIONPRENEUR®
PUBLISHING

Bring It On
Copyright © 2024 Dhiren Harchandani
First published in 2024

Print: 978-1-76124-099-7
E-book: 978-1-76124-120-8
Hardback: 978-1-76124-141-3

Publishing information
Publishing and design facilitated by Passionpreneur Publishing
A division of Passionpreneur Organization Pty Ltd
ABN: 48640637529

Melbourne, VIC | Australia
www.PassionpreneurPublishing.com

TABLE OF CONTENTS

FOREWORD

A na Fi Intizarak, 'Kindling the fire of curiosity'.

After countless evenings strolling along Edgware Road, I had grown accustomed to the delightful tapestry of sounds and aromas that emanated from the myriad of restaurants and bars. A sound that tickled my ears on this particular evening was the singing of Egypt's great Oum Kalthoum. It was a great way to kill time as I waited for my dinner guest to join me.

Dhiren, now living in Dubai, grew up in the Philippines, where he completed his schooling before moving to the United States to complete his formal education. The university education set him up for his first job in Silicon Valley, where he did exceptionally well. Hankering for change and adventure, Dhiren moved from San Francisco to Dubai with his wife, Jasmine.

Two years later, he had his hands full running a successful startup in the IT services field. As a side hustle, he got involved in the property market, and through family circumstances, he assisted with managing his in-law's multinational clothing company. Getting to know Dhiren, I saw his adeptness at juggling multiple balls simultaneously.

A guiding hand in the desert.

My first trip to Dubai was to open an investment office in the Dubai International Financial District. The boom was in full swing, and everyone was cashing in and getting fabulously (though some only on paper).

An old friend from the UK Midlands, whom I knew to be a heavyweight investor in the UAE, introduced me to his local business partner, Dhiren Harchandani, AKA Dhee, to get some insights into the country.

It was November 2009, at the beginning of the economic downturn, when Nakheel, a prominent developer, defaulted on its loans, sending ripples of fear throughout the country. I met with Dhiren to discuss the situation, which led to us investing in entities where we liked the character and credit: companies like Nakheel, Tamweel and Dubai Holdings, gambling on the UAE and its people. Ultimately, it turned out to be a good crisis, and the investments proved successful.

Dhiren's greatest asset was his character. Generous with his time, advice and help, he became a close friend, guide and counselor.

The saying, *Show me your teachers, and I will tell you who you are* bears testimony to Dhiren's role of teacher, counselor, and life coach when I needed one. It comes so naturally to him as he generously gives of himself, influencing those within his locus of control, which extends to his family, friends, employees, associates and later to mentees at the Entrepreneurs Organization, where he is an essential player.

Watching, listening and learning.

Observing the man on multiple business trips together, I learned about his non-negotiable routine: rising at 4:00am to meditate, exercise before breakfast, and tackle the day. After dinner, he retires to bed at 10:00pm and repeats the routine the next day, arriving at breakfast composed and ready to make significant decisions. He spends the day maintaining solid communication despite his full schedule. He purposefully cuts through the pressure, stress, and complexity, and delivers simple, effective results every time. Combined with his consistent routines, Dhiren is cautious about his food selection, which complements his exercise schedule to provide positive energy.

That is the man—Dhiren.

I am a work-in-progress trying to emulate his example. The two main areas I have not mastered are meditation and alcohol absti- nence. Experiencing Dhiren's entrepreneurial genius in action, his insight and confidence in conducting business, always amazes me. An example that comes to mind as I write is of a business he purchased and spent two years building up to become a strong competitor in its sector. The principal competitor was heading for disaster, which meant an increase in market share for Dhiren. He, however, sold the business. When I asked why, he simply stated that the offer to purchase was very attractive and it was time for everyone to move on. Without hesitation or indecision, he moved on with a clear vision to face the next challenge.

"Failure gives birth to success. Success breeds hubris and complacency."

Dhiren was part of a failed joint venture, partly due to the CEO of the UK partner not heeding Dhiren's sound advice about doing business in the Middle East. The CEO and founder of the company returned Dhiren's investment in full, acknowledging Dhiren's honorable conduct and contributions beyond the call of duty. Dhiren had taken the high ground, making good moral and business decisions, and his partners noticed and appreciated it.

We have grown as close as brothers since that first meeting, sharing life together. Some of the conversations we have had over the years play over in my head from time to time: *"Dhiren, why would you invest in something as uncertain as XYZ?"* I'd ask.

"You know, sometimes you're at the beach, and there's a wave. It's small, but if you wait patiently, a bigger one will come. When it does, and if you time it right, you can ride it for fun and profit. Deep down, you know it's destined to crash along the shore, but with your eyes open, you can ride the wave and enjoy it. You can keep an eye out to jump off before it hits the shore."

And this one: *"Dhiren, I met this girl."*

"That's great news!"

Then a few hours later, over dinner, he says: *"So, do you also like her as a person?"*

Another time, regarding a business opportunity, I said: *"Dhiren, the beauty of the business is that it's been around for fifty years, run by the same family, has never taken on any debt, and is the only company of its kind in the country with the lowest costs."*

"Can you trust them? How have they treated their minority partners in the last fifty years?"

The greatest thing one human can do for another is help them learn. Gurus, teachers, coaches—whatever they may be—are highly esteemed due to the power of this simple truth. They can give a man a fish and feed him, but they can choose to teach him to catch his own fish to feed himself, his family, and his village.

A few years ago, Dhiren told me about his decision to become a coach. He sold his remaining business and scaled down his new ventures to spend most, if not all, of his time coaching. My gut instinct was: Coaching, really? I was surprised and not sure what to make of it—even though there was no doubt in my mind, after two years of watching him, that he was a natural teacher.

I had accompanied him on Saturday mornings to help feed construction workers in Dubai, but this charity work was on evenings and weekends only. Coaching would be all day, every day. So, I wondered if 'coach' was code for a new startup that he would sell for an enormous profit in the second year. Could it scale up to become a platform, I asked? He laughed and answered that was not the plan. It would simply be one-to-one coaching. I realized Dhiren was being true to his nature—doing what he loved, not saving it for some time in the future.

It is easy to see he loves it and has the time of his life doing it. I sense his energy and passion. There can be no other way for Dhiren.

His impact on my life is immeasurable on all levels. He nudged me off the high diving board to plunge into a fulfilling life, creating my own family, for which I am eternally grateful. Frequent visits with *his* family helped me understand that without a healthy Inner Game, the Outer Game is all in vain.

One can only be eternally grateful for those who come into our lives, help us raise our game, and illuminate our path to be the best we can be.

I hope this book will help illuminate *your* path, too.

Marcus T.B. Verus, April 2022

DEDICATION

To my dearest family,

In the story of my life, each one of you is not just a chapter, but the very essence of the narrative. Your enduring love and unwavering support have filled the pages of my existence with profound warmth and joy.

Through life's unpredictable twists and turns, you've stood as my unyielding pillars, providing strength and solace in every storm. In your presence, I've learned the invaluable lessons of unconditional love and the priceless treasure that is family unity. As we continue to pen this remarkable story together, I'm grateful for each shared moment and the remarkable love that defines us as a family.

CHAPTER 1

WILL THE REAL ME PLEASE STAND UP!

BRING
IT
ON

"Change your vibe, change your life."

— DHIREN HARCHANDANI

Do you ever feel like you're a bird with clipped wings? Like you have the potential to soar, but you're being held back by something?

I used to feel like that all the time. I was my own greatest critic, constantly giving myself a one-star review and wondering why I wasn't an Oscar-winning actor in this grand production called *Life*. But hey, even Leonardo DiCaprio had his Titanic moments.

One day, amidst my melodrama, I hit rock bottom.

I had a reality check, and it wasn't a fun-filled vacation in the Bahamas. It hit me like a rogue wave—maybe the problem wasn't me, but the way I was scripting my own sitcom of self-deprecation.

So, I decided to eavesdrop on my inner voice, and boy, was it a drama queen. It was like having Shakespeare whispering insults in my ear, questioning my worth and painting a masterpiece of self-doubt. But I wasn't about to let my own mind play director in this tragicomedy of errors.

I embarked on a linguistic mission, armed with puns and a pinch of sass. I started replacing those negative scripts with uplifting punchlines. Instead of "I'm not good enough", I told myself, "I'm as legendary as Michael Jordan soaring through the air, dunking effortlessly!" This approach worked, until it didn't.

There was more to it than "positive self-talk".

I had to play the lead actor in my own rom-com.

Confidence had to become my co-star, and progress had to become my supporting cast.

I had to find that hidden treasure chest in the attic.

So, if you're tired of playing a minor role in the theater of self-doubt, it's time to grab that spotlight and deliver an Oscar-worthy performance. Let's rewrite the script, add some humor, and create a blockbuster called, "Bring it On!"

Popcorn, anyone?

CHANGE YOUR INNER GAME TO CHANGE YOUR LIFE

I was trapped in a common destructive pattern of negative self-talk. It was like having a stand-up comedian in your head, but instead of delivering hilarious punchlines, you are being bombarded with self-doubt and insecurity. Talk about a comedy club gone wrong!

This slowly eroded my confidence, intuition, and self-worth. As an entrepreneur and leader, this was especially damaging.

It was only then that I began to understand the significant role that the Inner Game plays in shaping our perspective and guiding our decisions. The Inner Game is the ongoing conversation we have with ourselves in the privacy of our minds. This conversation shapes the lens we rely on to make sense of the world around us. It can either empower or undermine us.

Along the way, we tend to forget that this is our show, our masterpiece: We should be grabbing that microphone, taking center stage, and letting our Inner Game guide us to success.

THE POWER OF
THE INNER GAME

The thoughts and words you use to describe yourself can have a powerful impact on your life. A negative inner dialogue can make you feel like you're not good enough, no matter what you do. It can lead to a lack of confidence, motivation, and happiness. It can also make it difficult to achieve your goals.

On the other hand, a positive inner dialogue can boost your self-esteem, help you stay motivated, and make it easier to reach your goals. When you challenge negative thoughts and replace them with positive ones, you can start to see yourself in a more positive light. And when you focus on your strengths and what you are good at, you will start to feel more confident and capable.

Therefore, it is paramount to pay attention to our internal dialogue, and to work on cultivating a positive Inner Game to achieve success on our own terms.

A SELF-IMPOSED PRISON

Our minds are constantly talking to us. Sometimes, this inner dialogue is positive and empowering. It can tell us things like, *You can do it!*, *You have a great business,* or *You have a great team—they think you're a great leader.*

However, for some people, the inner dialogue is negative and self-defeating. It can be like a crazy roommate from hell, constantly telling us we're not good enough, we'll never be successful, and we don't belong.

This negative self-talk can be a self-imposed prison. It can keep us from taking risks, trying new things, and achieving our goals. It can make us feel trapped and hopeless.

The incessant chatter of negative self-talk can lead to a self-imposed prison where one doesn't even see the bars.

LIFE BEFORE DISCOVERING THE INNER GAME

I used to have a nagging sense of unease about myself. It followed me around, and I couldn't help but feel like there was something wrong with me. As a result, I felt like a vital part of myself was slowly eroding away. I felt like I was losing a piece of myself, bit by bit.

I would have fleeting thoughts of self-doubt that I would brush off without giving them a second thought. But these thoughts were often so subtle that I didn't even notice that my negative self-talk was being etched into my psyche, slowly eroding my confidence, my innate intuition, and my sense of self-worth. It's a vicious cycle from which it can be difficult to break out without a clear understanding of the underlying code driving the narrative.

This constant cycle of negative self-talk and the pressure to succeed took a toll on my mental health and well-being. As an entrepreneur and leader, I was always striving for more. But this pursuit of MORE led to a depletion of my Inner Game, and I sacrificed my business, health, and relationships.

THE DESTRUCTIVE PURSUIT OF MORE

As an entrepreneur and leader, I also felt the pressure to succeed was immense. I believed that working harder and longer would bring me fulfillment and a sense of accomplishment. But instead, it depleted me and aged my body prematurely. My Outer Game appeared great, but I was sacrificing my Inner Game, putting my business, health, and relationships on the line.

I was chasing MORE—and in the process, I was destroying myself. The constant desire to have more, be more, and make more left me depleted and with nothing left for my inner self.

I owned a house on the golf course and a sports car was parked in my driveway, but I was homeless and I felt stuck. I had a loving wife and a child on the way, but I felt alone and isolated.

I eventually realized that my Inner Game was playing a crucial role in both my success and my struggles. When I focused on my Inner Game, I was able to achieve success without sacrificing my health, relationships, or happiness. But when I neglected my Inner Game, I was headed for disaster.

THE MOMENT OF TRUTH

The inner conversation is like a self-talk radio station that is always broadcasting in our heads, a broadcast which can make or break us. Just like a radio station, our inner conversation is constantly propagating a variety of messages. Some of these messages are helpful and supportive, while others are negative and critical. The challenge is to learn how to tune out the negative messages and focus on the positive ones.

As a young consultant in the tech Mecca, I relied on my Inner Game to scale my career while burning the midnight oil with Fortune 500 companies and startups. I was the master of my domain, or so I thought. But lurking beneath the surface of my success were self-doubt, stress, anxiety, and mental fatigue. It was like a twisted game of Whack-A-Mole, where every achievement came with a pounding dose of impostor syndrome.

And let's not forget the desperate attempts to fit in socially. I mean, who needs a supportive Inner Game when you have alcohol, right? Alcohol was my secret weapon to feel socially accepted and connected.

But life has a funny way of waking us up, often quite literally. I remember one day I woke up in bed and told my wife that I didn't have long to live. My heart was racing, and I was convinced that I was going to die young. I dragged myself to countless doctors, who gave me puzzled looks and shrugged their shoulders. "It's all in your head," they said, as if that helped calm my racing heart.

Armed with determination and a dash of desperation, I decided to take matters into my own hands. I embarked on a quest for self-help and self-development. Books became my trusty side-kicks, workshops my secret training grounds, and masterclasses my enlightening boot camps.

Imagine me, a former Silicon Valley consultant who had turned into a self-help junkie. I was surrounded by books; my journal was filled with frantic scribblings. Some of my friends were deeply concerned, but I was simply trying to figure out how to navigate the labyrinth of my own mind.

THE POWER OF BRUTAL HONESTY

I had been practicing positive self-talk, self-care, and resilience, but I found that the changes I made were often fleeting and didn't bring me the long-lasting transformation that I craved. I realized that I needed to go deeper.

I had to go beyond what was being espoused in the mainstream culture. Practicing "positive self-talk", "self-care", and "resilience" was a great foundation, but it wasn't bringing me sustainable changes. I had to go beyond these to get to the root. I had to ask myself the hard questions. That was the only way.

CONFRONTING DEEPLY ROOTED BELIEFS

I had to confront my deeply rooted beliefs and reframe my understanding of resilience, focus, empowerment, and habits. For example, I used to believe that resilience meant bouncing back from adversity without any emotional response. But I learned that resilience actually involves feeling and processing difficult emotions, not just ignoring them.

Another misconception I previously held was that focus meant completely blocking out distractions and maintaining intense concentration for extended periods. However, research indicates that our brains function best when we establish a rhythm involving regular breaks and micro-moments of recovery for stretching and resetting. Instead of trying to eliminate distractions entirely, it's more effective to develop strategies for managing them.

After learning that I needed to go deeper, I began to confront my deeply rooted beliefs about resilience, focus, empowerment, and habits. I had to learn how to recognize and reframe the myths I held about these topics. This was a challenging process, but it was essential if I wanted to achieve sustainable personal growth.

I discovered that many of us fail to get to the root of our problems, preferring instead to address surface-level issues. This can lead to a lack of sustainable change and frustration in our personal growth journey.

EMPOWERMENT FROM WITHIN

Achieving true empowerment and sustainable personal growth is not easy. Many of us struggle to liberate from the limiting beliefs and societal expectations that hold us back, and the journey can be filled with setbacks and challenges.

THE REALITY

I was tired of feeling stuck in the same place day after day, year after year. Research shows that over seventy percent of people who consciously attempt to transform themselves will fail. That means the majority of us are, and will continue, living the same unfulfilling lives, day in and day out.

Why? This was the tough question that I had to ask myself before I could truly start making progress on my journey to personal growth.

After realizing that achieving true empowerment is not easy, I began to explore the reasons why so many of us resist change and accept stagnation in our lives.

I was curious to know why so many people are not achieving their goals, not living up to their potential, and not reaching the heights they know they're capable of.

Why do we resist change for the safety of mediocrity?

Why do we keep finding ourselves in the same place today as we were yesterday?

Why do we accept stagnation?

We have all been conditioned to believe certain narratives about ourselves and our capabilities, but these limiting beliefs can hold us back from achieving our full potential. In this book, I will peel back the layers to help you get to the answers that lie within you.

To truly transform, it was essential that I develop the "Bring It On" mindset. I had to ask myself the tough questions.

- Why do I resist change for the safety of mediocrity?

- What limiting beliefs that are holding me back?

- What are my goals?

- What are the steps I need to take to achieve my goals?

- What are the challenges I will face along the way?

- How will I overcome these challenges?

- Why do I keep finding myself in the same place today as I was yesterday?

- Why do I accept stagnation?

- What kind of person have I been?

- What kind of person do I present to the world?

- What kind of person am I really like inside?

- Is there a feeling that I experience and struggle with over and over again?

- Which part of my personality do I need to improve?

- What is the one thing I want to change about myself?

- Why do I accept the limiting beliefs that I have been conditioned to believe?

It was time to face the truth.

THE INNER GAME BLUEPRINT

As an entrepreneur, I've faced my fair share of challenges. One of the biggest challenges I faced was that relentless inner voice that constantly whispered, "You're just not good enough." I felt like I was constantly battling my own self-doubt, and it was starting to hold me back.

But then I found the key to sustainable transformation: the Inner Game blueprint. This blueprint helped me to silence that inner voice and to focus on my strengths. It was my guiding light, the beacon that helped me navigate the stormy seas of self-doubt. And I'm here to share it with you in this book.

Within these pages, I invite you on a journey through my entrepreneurial adventures, where I unravel the secrets behind this game-changing blueprint. I'll share with you the tools and techniques that I applied to overcome my self-doubt and to achieve my goals.

I've faced some pretty fierce waves. But with the help of the Inner Game blueprint, I was able to weather the storm and to emerge stronger.

You see, this blueprint wasn't handed to me on a silver platter. It was forged in the fires of adversity, honed through countless struggles, and refined through determination. It became my lifeline, providing me with the strength and willpower to push forward, even when reality seemed to conspire against me.

Here's the exciting part: This book isn't just about my experiences. It's a treasure trove of interventions, strategies, and insights that I've acquired and developed during my own battles. I've compiled them all here, ready for you to embrace and apply to your own life.

I firmly believe that your struggles and hardships have the power to birth your purpose. It's in those darkest moments wherein you find the fuel to ignite your true calling.

MY WHY (PURPOSE)

I believe a business can be a profound force for good in our societies, communities, cities, and the world.

This force for good starts and ends with an entrepreneur who takes a balanced approach between profit and lifestyle.

My approach as a catalyst of transformation will serve as the foundation for our future generations to live healthier and more fulfilling lives. I believe entrepreneurs should be able to live a balanced lifestyle, while still growing successful, impactful businesses.

"Self-belief is an unfair advantage: not everyone has it."

— DHIREN HARCHANDANI

CONCLUSION

The Inner Game is an essential part of success. If you can master your thoughts and beliefs, the Outer Game becomes easier. Self-belief is an unfair advantage: Not everyone has it.

In the next chapter, we will explore how you can make a small shift in your Inner Game that will dissolve problems you're trying to solve. We will dive deeper into understanding your internal narrative, identifying limiting beliefs, and recoding them, which will serve as the foundation to your Inner Game.

NOTE TO READER

By sharing this personal narrative, I aim to connect your empathy to the broader understanding of the Inner Game's influence on our lives.

The tools and interventions at the end of each chapter are the foundation of the Inner Game blueprint. I have designed this book to be an experience that takes you through a transformation, using stories, interventions, and other exercises.

As you read, I encourage you to reflect on your own experiences and to experiment with the tools and interventions. The more you practice, the greater the results.

I believe that everyone has the potential to reach their highest potential. This book is my gift to you, to help you on your path.

INNER GAME BLUEPRINT

Our thoughts and beliefs shape our reality. If we have limiting beliefs, we will set limits on ourselves and our potential. But if we can identify our limiting beliefs and challenge them, we can open up a world of possibilities.

EXERCISE

- What are your limiting beliefs?
    - What do you believe about yourself that holds you back?
    - What do you believe about the world that makes you feel like you can't achieve your goals?

- What are your goals?

  ○ What do you want to achieve in life?

  ○ What are the specific steps you need to take to achieve your goals?

- How will you overcome the challenges you will face along the way?

  ○ What challenges do you think you will face on your journey to achieving your goals?

  ○ How will you overcome these challenges?

The answers to these questions are within you. All you have to do is open your mind and heart to the possibility of change. By identifying your limiting beliefs, setting goals, and planning how to overcome challenges, you will create a blueprint for success.

CHAPTER 2

FROM SOLVING TO DISSOLVING

BRING
IT
ON

*"Your most dangerous 'competitor'
is contaminated thinking."*

— DHIREN HARCHANDANI

This quote captures the essence of what this chapter is about. In this chapter, we will explore the power of reframing and the importance of challenging our limiting beliefs.

INTRODUCTION

Are negative thoughts and self-doubt holding you back? If so, you're not alone. But there is hope. We can learn to overcome these challenges and build our confidence.

Welcome to this chapter, where we will explore the art of reframing and how it can help us to solve problems and transform our mindset. Reframing is a powerful tool that can encourage us to see our problems in a new light. It can help us to challenge negative thoughts and adopt new perspectives.

Let's bring it on!

MY SELF-TALK AND ITS IMPACT

My Inner Voice has been a critical and negative force that hindered my full potential. It reinforced my limiting beliefs, such as I'm not smart enough or I'm not capable of achieving my goals. These beliefs became a self-fulfilling prophecy, preventing me from taking risks, pursuing dreams, and embracing new opportunities.

REFRAMING: UNLOCKING INFINITE POSSIBILITIES

Our thoughts have immense power. They can hold us back or propel us forward, limit our potential, or unleash our true greatness.

As I began to understand the impact of my Inner Voice, I discovered the powerful tool of reframing.

Reframing is the process of changing the way we think about a situation, event, or experience. By shifting our perspective, we can change the meaning we attach to it, which in turn affects our thoughts, feelings, and behaviors.

Reframing allowed me to view my challenges as opportunities, setbacks as learning experiences, and obstacles as stepping-stones toward growth. It empowered me to find hidden possibilities, embrace optimism, and develop a resourceful mindset.

Dr. Ethan Kross is a leading researcher in reframing and emotional regulation. In his 2021 book, *Chatter: The Voice in Our Head, Why It Matters, and How to Harness It*, he conducted numerous studies highlighting the benefits of reframing. His studies have shown that individuals who practice reframing experience better emotional regulation, increased resilience, and a greater sense of control over their lives.

REFRAMING SELF-DOUBT: SUMMITING MOUNT MERU AS A FAMILY

Picture this: The wind is howling, snowflakes are pelting your face, and your muscles are screaming for mercy. You're scaling Mount Meru, the fifth-highest mountain in Africa, in the most brutal weather conditions imaginable. It's like Mother Nature herself decided to crank up the difficulty level just for kicks. But hey, why not throw in some extra challenges, right?

Now, in the midst of this icy chaos, there's my son Mikhayl, battling not only the elements but also a nasty case of self-doubt. The little guy was questioning his every step, wondering if he had what it took to conquer this beast of a mountain.

But then, in a stroke of genius, our guide Yaseen stepped in with a dose of inspiration. He looked at Mikhayl and said, "Hey, imagine this, my friend. Imagine yourself standing tall at the summit, basking in the glory of being the youngest climber I've ever guided to conquer Mount Meru." Talk about a game-changer!

That simple act of reframing shifted Mikhayl's entire perspective. He went from doubting himself to envisioning the incredible feat he could achieve. Suddenly, his focus shifted from his perceived limitations to his untapped potential. He tapped into his inner reservoir of strength and determination, powering through the challenges like a boss. And guess what? He actually reached that summit, defying the odds and making us all proud.

That experience was a wake-up call for all of us. It opened our eyes to the mighty power of reframing. It taught me that our thoughts can either be our biggest obstacle or our greatest ally. And even when life throws its most insane challenges at us, we have the ability to change our perspective, rise above the chaos, and conquer our own mountains.

UNLEASHING THE POWER OF TRANSFORMED BELIEFS

We all have limiting beliefs that hold us back. These beliefs can be about our abilities, our worth, or our place in the world. They can be rooted in our childhood experiences, our cultural conditioning, or our own negative self-talk.

But what if we could transform these limiting beliefs? What if we could reframe our beliefs and see ourselves in a new light?

When we transform our beliefs, we change our reality. We become architects of our destiny, guided by unwavering conviction and armed with the tools to transform adversity into triumph.

THE SIGNIFICANCE OF THE INNER GAME

My Outer Game achievements were important, but they were merely the byproduct of my Inner Game.

The Inner Game is the realm of our thoughts, emotions, and beliefs. It is the foundation of our Outer Game performance.

When we focus on our Inner Game, we are able to identify and transform our limiting beliefs. We become more aware of our thoughts and emotions, and we learn how to manage them.

AN AWAKENING TO THE POWER OF CHANGE

My limiting beliefs held me back for a long time, but then I had an awakening. I realized that I could rewrite my story and challenge these limiting beliefs.

It was like a veil had been lifted. I could see the self-imposed barriers that had been holding me back for so long. I felt a surge of emotions—frustration, determination, and a flicker of hope. I was ready to change my life.

UNCOVERING THE ORIGINS: REWRITING THE HISTORY WITHIN

I began to explore my past with the hope of understanding how my limiting beliefs had originated. I realized that many of these beliefs were based on negative experiences that I'd had as a child. But I also realized that I could rewrite my history. I could choose to see these experiences in a new light.

I started to practice introspection and reframing. I asked myself questions, like "What did I learn from this experience?" and "How can I use this experience to grow?" I began to see my past in a new light, and I started to feel empowered.

A HEARTFELT DECISION

Our journey commences with an extraordinary chapter in my life. As fate would have it, my family's relocation from India to the Philippines when I was a baby set the stage for a heartfelt decision that would shape my childhood.

THE RIPPLE EFFECT OF AN UNCONVENTIONAL ARRANGEMENT

Shortly after we moved to the Philippines, my parents made a self-less decision to have me live with my aunt and uncle who were having difficulty conceiving a child at that point. I was a toddler and didn't understand why I was leaving them. I felt scared and alone, but my aunt and uncle were loving and supportive. I grew up feeling like I was part of two worlds, missing my parents and sister.

SEEDS OF LIMITING BELIEFS

As a young child, I unknowingly internalized the unconventional arrangement of living with my aunt and uncle. I perceived them as my biological parents.

However, a few years later, my aunt and uncle welcomed a child of their own. This was a miraculous turn of events, but it also meant that I would have to return to live with my biological parents.

I was confused and heartbroken by this sudden change. I didn't understand why I had to leave my aunt and uncle and, subconsciously, I felt like I was being abandoned once again.

These experiences left me with the seeds of limiting beliefs about myself.

UNRAVELING THE PATTERNS

I began to believe that I was not good enough to be loved.

The impact of my unconventional upbringing reverberated throughout my journey, impacting my relationships, academic performance, and overall well-being. As I grew into adulthood, I discovered recurring patterns of feeling unsafe and insecure. These patterns unknowingly sabotaged my relationships, as I was constantly on the lookout for signs of abandonment. The looming threat of abandonment had woven its threads deep within my being.

RELATIONSHIPS

In my relationships and friendships, I often found myself feeling unsettled and anxious. I was constantly worried that I would be abandoned, and I would often act out in ways that pushed them away.

ACADEMIC PERFORMANCE

My academic performance also suffered as a result of my insecurity. I was afraid of failure, and I would often procrastinate on assignments or avoid difficult tasks. I also found it difficult to focus in class, as I was always worrying about what might happen if I didn't do well.

WELL-BEING

My overall well-being also declined as a result of my unconventional upbringing. I often felt I didn't belong and was anxious as a result.

These limiting beliefs have had a profound impact on my life. They have held me back from my potential.

A REVELATION AT THE WORKSHOP

So, there I was, attending this workshop with my buddy Chezard, ready to dive into the depths of my inner world. It was like a therapy session, but with a lot more soul-searching and a lot less awkward silence.

As I delved into the recesses of my mind, it hit me like a ton of bricks (not literally, thankfully). My childhood experiences had played a sneaky game of mind control, shaping my beliefs about myself and the world.

I realized I had been lugging around pain and fear like an over-packed suitcase on a never-ending journey. No wonder I couldn't fully embrace life's adventures. I was too busy tripping over my own emotional baggage.

But then Robert, the intervention guru, entered the scene. He had a knack for untangling the mess of limiting beliefs. He was like a mental detective, sniffing out every belief that had hitched a ride into my psyche. And boy, did I have a whole convoy of them!

It turns out, I had collected not one, not ten, but a whopping twenty-seven limiting beliefs along the bumpy road of my childhood. It was like a tangled web of thoughts, all intricately woven into the fabric of my being. Talk about baggage overload!

That workshop was a turning point for me. It was like I had stumbled upon hidden treasure: the key to my own liberation. I realized I held the power to change my life, to rewrite the narrative that had been playing on repeat, for far too long.

Gone were the days of blaming my circumstances for my problems. It was time to step up, take charge, and embark on a journey of self-responsibility. I had to become the hero of my own healing, armed with a toolbox of empowerment and a determination to set myself free.

REVELATIONS SHARED

I was apprehensive, yet hopeful as I shared the profound revelations and insights I had gained from the NLP workshop with my parents. This pivotal moment marked the beginning of a journey of vulnerability and healing. As I opened up about the childhood experiences that had shaped my Inner Game, a sacred space of understanding and empathy emerged. Their unwavering support became the driving force for transformation, laying the groundwork for powerful reframing.

REFRAMING THE PAST

I shared with my parents the profound discoveries I had made, including twenty-seven limiting beliefs that were intricately tied to my childhood experiences. They swiftly reframed those experiences, revealing a truth that resonated deep within my soul. They lovingly explained that I was the missing puzzle piece that made their family complete. This empowering reframe shifted my perspective, allowing me to shed the weight of those limiting beliefs that had once defined me. While I may never have absolute certainty, I choose to embrace the narrative that empowers me, that celebrates my worth and resilience.

THE DEPTH OF REFRAMING

Reframing childhood experiences is not about denying or invalidating negative emotions. Instead, it is an invitation to honor and explore them with compassion and curiosity. This allows for a broader perspective, one that acknowledges the challenges while seeking the lessons and opportunities that can be found within them. Reframing is a transformative process that fosters personal evolution, and serves as a testament to the resilience of the human spirit.

CONCLUSION: EMBRACING THE MAGIC OF REFRAMING

In conclusion, the power of reframing is real. We can choose to see challenges as opportunities, setbacks as learning experiences, and obstacles as footholds to growth. As Ralph Waldo Emerson said, "The only person you are destined to become is the person you decide to be."

Throughout this chapter, we have delved into the art of reframing, and problem dissolution.

We have learned that our most dangerous "competitor" is contaminated thinking, and that reframing is the key to unlocking infinite possibilities.

KEY LESSONS AND TAKEAWAYS INCLUDE:

- The power of reframing: By changing our perspective, we can change the meaning we attach to situations, events, and experiences, leading to a shift in our thoughts, feelings, and behaviors.

- Transforming limiting beliefs: We have the ability to rewrite our limiting beliefs and see ourselves in a new light. This empowers us to overcome challenges, pursue our goals, and embrace our worth and resilience.

- The impact of the Inner Game: Our thoughts, emotions, and beliefs shape our Outer Game performance. By focusing on our Inner Game, we can identify and transform limiting beliefs, manage our thoughts and emotions, and become more resilient.

- Unraveling the patterns: Exploring the origins of our limiting beliefs helps us understand how they have influenced our lives. Through introspection and reframing, we can let go of self-doubt, rewrite our history, and embrace personal growth.

- The ripple effect of reframing: Reframing has a profound impact on our relationships, opportunities, and sense of purpose. It allows us to reclaim our power, rewrite our stories, and align with our true potential.

As we embrace reframing, we are invited to honor and explore our negative emotions with compassion and curiosity, seeking lessons and opportunities within challenges. This transformative process fosters personal evolution and serves as a testament to the resilience of the human spirit.

INTERVENTION

The Inner Game Blueprint: Rewriting Your Narrative

Let's take a moment to explore some of your narratives.

This forms the basis for identifying your Inner Game.

Do a brief synopsis of your family relationships—with your parents, brothers, and sisters. Note any significant impacts on your life, positive or negative, then and now.

_____

_____

Considering the negative impacts on your life, think deeply about them before answering the following questions and elaborating.

What do you specifically remember?

_____

_____

Is it true?

_____

_____

Why?

_____

_____

Have you verified this with a parent, sibling, or other?

_____

_____

How were they impacted?

_____

_____

Do you need help clearing these thoughts up?

_____

_____

Are you willing to do whatever it takes to get to the bottom of it?

_____

_____

INTERVENTION
The Inner Game Blueprint: Reframing Beliefs

One of the easiest interventions used for limiting beliefs is called "reframing." Reframing involves shifting your perspective and looking at a situation or belief from a different angle. Here's a step-by-step guide on how to apply reframing as an intervention for limiting beliefs:

1. Identify the limiting belief. What is the belief that is holding you back? Write it down or say it out loud.

2. Challenge the belief. Is this belief based on facts, or just your perception? What evidence do you have to support or contradict the belief?

3. Find alternative interpretations. How else could you interpret the situation or belief? What would a more empowering interpretation be?

4. Gather evidence. Think of times in your past when you have successfully challenged similar beliefs or achieved things that contradicted your limiting belief. What evidence can you gather to support the new interpretation?

5. Create empowering affirmations. Develop positive and empowering statements that counteract the limiting belief. Write them down and repeat them to yourself regularly.

6. Visualize success. Imagine yourself successfully overcoming the limiting belief and achieving your goals. What does it look like? How do you feel?

7. Take action. Take steps that align with the new empowering belief. Challenge yourself to engage in activities or experiences that prove your belief wrong and help you build evidence of your capabilities.

Remember, reframing takes practice and persistence. It's essential to consistently reinforce the new empowering belief and challenge the old limiting belief whenever it arises. Over time, with consistent effort, you can rewire your thought patterns and replace limiting beliefs with more empowering ones.

Here are some additional tips for reframing limiting beliefs:

- Be patient and kind to yourself. It takes time to change your beliefs, so don't get discouraged if you don't see results immediately.

- Be willing to experiment. There is no one right way to reframe a belief, so try different techniques and see what works best for you.

- Have fun! Reframing can be a challenging but rewarding process. Enjoy the journey of discovering your true potential.

CHAPTER 3

CHANGING LANES

The One Habit that Dissolved
Seventeen Problems

BRING
IT
ON

"All beliefs and behavior are learned and can therefore be unlearned."

— STANISLAV GROF, CZECH-BORN PSYCHIATRIST

UNLEASHING THE POWER OF HABIT TRANSFORMATION

In today's fast-paced world, personal growth and success are like those fancy combo meals—you can't just have the talent and hard work, you have to upgrade your habits too!

It's time for a habit revolution!

Join me for an intriguing and surprising journey ahead. We're about to explore the powerful impact of changing just one tiny habit.

I know it may sound surprising—but believe me, it sets off a chain-reaction with substantial consequences.

Picture this: As we take that leap of faith and transform that one key habit, the barriers that have been holding us back will break down. It's like finding a quick and easy way to achieve our goals.

Eventually, opportunities will present themselves, and we'll make progress in all areas of our lives. One habit at a time, we can break free from the constraints of mediocrity and embark on a journey where success is within reach.

This journey is about to rock your socks off!

THE REPETITIVE CYCLE

The repetitive cycle is a three-step process that involves a trigger, a response, and reinforcement. The trigger is an event, thought, or emotion that initiates an unproductive pattern of behavior. The response is the behavior that is triggered. The reinforcement is the outcome of the response that makes it more likely to happen again.

In my journey, the trigger to my alcohol habit was often social situations where alcohol was present. The response was to drink alcohol as a way to cope with stress or social pressure. The reinforcement was the perceived benefits of drinking, such as relaxation and confidence in social situations.

The repetitive cycle can be a powerful force in our lives. It can keep us stuck in unhealthy habits and prevent us from achieving our goals. However, once we understand the cycle, we can start to break it.

RECOGNIZING
SELF-DESTRUCTIVE PATTERNS

Self-destructive patterns held me back from achieving my goals. My patterns took many forms, such as negative self-talk, procrastination, and addiction. Leaving these patterns unchecked hindered my progress and limited my potential.

The silver lining is that once I became aware of my patterns, I could start taking steps to change them. I started challenging my negative self-talk, and I found healthy ways to cope with my stress. By shining a light on these patterns and understanding their impact, I gained a deeper level of self-awareness which amplified my self-empowerment.

THE CONSEQUENCES OF MY ACTIONS

During my transition from college to the real world, I was overwhelmed by the weight of expectations and the battle with my mental well-being. I turned to alcohol as a crutch to alleviate my anxieties.

Naively, I convinced myself that two drinks wouldn't impair my ability to drive. With a false sense of confidence, I got behind the wheel after consuming alcohol. The darkened streets blurred before my eyes as the effects of alcohol seeped into my consciousness.

Racing thoughts, an inability to focus, and a distorted perception overcame me as I drove under the influence. At that moment, the consequences of my actions were far from my mind.

HITTING ROCK BOTTOM

Moments later, a piercing siren shattered the illusion of invincibility. Dread washed over me like a tidal wave as a police officer signaled for me to pull over. It was in that instant, standing there in the face of impending consequences, that the realization of the importance of my choices struck me like a lightning bolt.

THE SEEDS OF ESCAPE
FROM ALCOHOL

Amidst the stark reality of my predicament, a profound realization washed over me. It became abundantly clear that the fleeting escape alcohol had promised was nothing more than an illusory trap. The attempt to alleviate stress and anxiety only intensified these very emotions. This quote echoed in my mind:

"Drinking alcohol to relieve stress or anxiety doesn't work. Usually, one ends up with both more stress and more anxiety."

— DR. GABOR MATÉ

My mind raced with the potential outcomes and what my parents would have to say, or my boss if he found out I have a police record.

From that moment on, a profound shift took place within my being. Fear and regret coursed through my veins.

SHADOWS OF MISTAKES

The aftermath of that fateful night forced me to confront the consequences of my actions and acknowledge the self-destructive cycle I had unknowingly perpetuated. It was a painful reckoning, but within the shadows of my mistakes, I discovered a glimmer of hope.

THE FIRST STEP TOWARDS TRANSFORMATION

In our pursuit of personal transformation, we often hope that extreme situations will serve as powerful catalysts for change. However, even such extreme situations can fall short of providing long-lasting motivation. True transformation requires a deeper understanding of ourselves and a genuine readiness to embrace change.

As James Gordon astutely observed, "It's not that some people have willpower, and some don't. It's that some people are ready to change, and others are not." This recognition underscores the vital importance of assessing our readiness before embarking on the transformative journey.

A SOLEMN COMMITMENT

I made a commitment to free myself from the clutches of those destructive patterns and embark on a journey of self-reflection, growth, and healing. I set out to unravel the complexities of my habits and dismantle the cycle that had held me captive.

Each day became an opportunity to cultivate self-awareness, exploring the underlying factors that drove me towards destructive habits. Through introspection, I gained insights into the triggers and emotional patterns that perpetuated the cycle.

ESCAPING THE GRIP OF AN UNHEALTHY HABIT

Breaking a long-ingrained habit can be challenging, but it is possible with the right strategies and tactics. In my case, I used a combination of fitness and meditation to help me change my alcohol habit.

Fitness helped me to release endorphins, which have mood-boosting effects. It also helped me to improve my self-esteem and confidence, which made me less likely to turn to alcohol as a way to cope with stress or negative emotions. Meditation helped me to become more aware of my thoughts and feelings, and learn how to respond to them in a non-reactive way. It also helped me to develop a sense of calm and peace, which made it easier for me to resist the urge to drink.

UNDERSTANDING THE CYCLE: TRIGGER, RESPONSE, REINFORCEMENT

To address the alcohol habit, it was crucial to understand the cycle of behaviors that perpetuated it. The cycle consisted of triggers, responses, and reinforcements.

- Triggers: Social situations where alcohol was present acted as triggers for my drinking habit.

- Responses: When triggered, I turned to alcohol as a coping mechanism, which provided temporary relief from stress or social pressure.

- Reinforcements: The perceived benefits of drinking, such as relaxation and confidence in social situations, reinforced the cycle and made it difficult to liberate.

Unfortunately, being aware of the cycle didn't bring immediate change. It took time to realize that this habit was the root cause of other issues in my life.

UNRAVELING THE HIDDEN IMPACT OF HABITS

I've spent a lot of time thinking about habits. It seems like everyone is struggling with one they want to break or adopt. I wondered why this is so common.

The answer shook me to my core. When one aspect of our lives isn't functioning optimally, it can create a chain reaction of fifteen to twenty problems. These problems can be minor or major, and some may be hidden from our conscious awareness.

What's even more striking is that many of these problems originate from the very habit we're trying to change. This means that transforming our habits can have a profound impact on our overall well-being. By changing a single habit, we have the potential to unravel a complex web of interconnected obstacles.

THE POWER OF CLARITY AND ASSESSMENT

To change my alcohol habit, I first needed to gain clarity on all the problems it was causing me. I identified seventeen distinct issues, both trivial and serious.

TRIVIAL PROBLEMS

- Frequent hangovers
- Increased spending on alcohol
- Unpleasant physical effects
- Difficulty maintaining a consistent sleep schedule.

- Decreased motivation and energy levels
- Impaired judgment and decision-making
- Neglect of hobbies and interests
- Strained relationships with friends and family
- Poor concentration and memory recall

SERIOUS PROBLEMS

- Risk of developing long-term health issues
- Impaired driving ability
- Increased susceptibility to mental health disorders
- Neglect of personal and professional responsibilities
- Deterioration of overall physical and mental well-being

By recognizing the full spectrum of problems associated with my alcohol habit, I realized that addressing it would have a profound and positive impact on my life.

QUANTIFYING THE TRUE COST

I wanted to understand the true cost of my alcohol habit, so I meticulously evaluated both the direct and indirect expenses. I also calculated the unproductive hours I lost after each drinking episode.

The cumulative toll alcohol took on my life was staggering. I was spending hundreds of dollars each month on alcohol, and I was losing an average of ten hours per week due to hangovers and other alcohol-related problems.

This newfound awareness gave me a powerful motivation to effect lasting change. I knew that I could not afford to continue living like this.

A DEFINING CHAPTER OF TRANSFORMATION

The night that police officer pulled me over changed everything. It became a defining chapter in my life. It taught me the importance of confronting our vulnerabilities head-on, and the transformative power found within a single moment of awakening. I carry its lessons with me as I navigate life's challenges and strive to live a more authentic and fulfilling existence.

Above all, the night that transformed everything taught me the importance of summoning the courage to face my shortcomings, acknowledge my mistakes, and embrace the journey of growth and self-discovery.

EMBRACING VULNERABILITY

Breaking a long-ingrained alcohol habit required vulnerability, self-reflection, and discipline. It took courage to confront uncomfortable truths about myself and my behavior. Admitting that alcohol provided a false sense of belonging, was challenging.

Vulnerability is essential for habit transformation. It allowed me to see my habit for what it really was. I had believed I used alcohol to help me to connect with others, but was I really connecting with them authentically?

When I was honest with myself about my habit, I began to understand the underlying reasons why I engaged in it. This understanding was essential for making lasting changes.

Vulnerability also allowed me to connect with those who were struggling with the same challenges. When I shared my story with them, I felt less alone and more supported. This support was invaluable when I was trying to make changes in my life.

A SLIPPERY MOMENT

One time, I was at a party, and I was feeling really tempted to drink. I had been sober for a few years, but I was feeling stressed and anxious. I thought about just having one drink, but I knew that it would be a slippery slope.

So, I decided to be vulnerable. I told my friend how I was feeling, and she was really supportive. She helped me to stay strong and to resist the temptation to drink.

I'm so grateful that I had the courage to be vulnerable that night. It helped me to stay sober, and it also helped me to build a stronger relationship with my friend.

NAVIGATING SOCIAL CIRCLES

Breaking the alcohol habit led to a smaller social circle, which I filled with new activities that supported my sobriety and well-being.

Social circles can be a powerful force for change, but they can also be a source of temptation. When I was trying to break my alcohol habit, I made changes to my social circles by spending less time with people who were not supportive of my goals, and engaging in new activities that were more aligned with my new lifestyle.

DISCOVERING A VIBRANT
AND ALIGNED SELF

Through new activities and lifestyle choices, I discovered a more vibrant, resilient, and aligned version of myself. While the loss of some social connections was painful, it ultimately paved the way for new and meaningful connections with people who supported my commitment to a healthier, alcohol-free lifestyle.

REFLECTIONS AND PERSONAL INSIGHTS

Looking back, alcohol had been a disruptive presence, even though I hadn't been a heavy drinker. It influenced my lifestyle, clouded my thinking, impacted my mood, and weakened my immune system.

What struck me the most was the subtle erosion of my self-esteem and self-worth after alcohol consumption. The days following alcohol consumption brought about a noticeable change in my thoughts, burdening my head with lingering effects.

Socializing under the influence of alcohol also revealed another aspect of its impact. Conversations lacked substance and depth, failing to reach the level of connection I desired.

These reflections led to a realization about the disruptive nature of alcohol in my life. They emphasized the importance of making conscious choices and understanding the true effects of our actions.

CONCLUSION: THE POWER OF BREAKING A HABIT

This chapter has shown that breaking a single key habit can have a profound impact on our lives. By understanding the cycle of behaviors, recognizing the hidden impact of habits, and quantifying the cost, we can liberate ourselves from old patterns and embark on a journey of personal growth.

If you are struggling with an unhealthy habit, don't wait any longer to break it. The quote by George Bernard Shaw, "The chains of habit are too light to be felt until they are too heavy to be broken," should motivate you to take action today. The longer you wait, the more difficult it will become.

BREAKING A HABIT

Two interventions are provided to assist in breaking a habit.

(1) Intervention #1: Inner Game Blueprint: Breaking the Cycle

- Identify the cycle of repetitive behaviors. This includes triggers, responses, and reinforcements. By understanding the cycle, individuals can liberate themselves by recognizing and interrupting unproductive patterns.

(2) Intervention #2: Inner Game Blueprint: Your one habit that dissolves your problems

- Assess your readiness for change, acknowledging the true cost of the habit and quantifying the problems associated with it. By understanding the full spectrum of issues caused by the habit, individuals can cultivate the mindset and determination required to embrace transformation.

INTERVENTION

① Inner Game Blueprint: Breaking the Cycle

Objective: The objective of this exercise is to help individuals recognize and understand their personal triggers, responses, and reinforcements that contribute to their repetitive cycle of unproductive behaviors. By gaining awareness of these patterns, individuals can begin the process of breaking free from them and creating positive change.

STEPS

1. Self-reflection: Take a few moments to reflect on your own life, and identify a specific behavior or habit that you find yourself repeatedly engaging in which hinders your progress or prevents you from reaching your true potential. It could be related to work, personal relationships, health, or any other area of your life.

2. Trigger identification: Now, think about the triggers that often lead you to engage in this behavior. What events, thoughts, or emotions typically set off this chain reaction? Write down at least three triggers that you have identified.

3. Response analysis: Next, analyze your typical responses to these triggers. How do you usually react or behave when faced with these triggers? Are there specific patterns or habits that you fall into? Write down your typical responses, ensuring that you're honest and open with yourself.

4. Reinforcement evaluation: Reflect on the rewards or perceived benefits that you derive from engaging in these behaviors, even if they are counterproductive in the long run. What do you gain or temporarily avoid by responding in this way? Write down the reinforcements that you associate with your responses.

5. Reflection and insights: Take a step back and review the triggers, responses, and reinforcements you have identified. What patterns or connections do you notice? Are there any common themes or underlying factors contributing to this cycle? Reflect on how this cycle has affected your progress and potential.

6. Action plan: Based on your insights, brainstorm other, more productive responses that you can adopt when faced with these triggers. Consider strategies, techniques, or new habits that can break the cycle and move you closer to your desired outcome. Write down your action plan, including specific steps you can take to implement these changes.

Remember, liberating yourself from this cycle takes time and effort. Be patient with yourself and commit to practicing the new responses and behaviors consistently. By doing so, you can gradually transform your habits and unlock your true potential.

INTERVENTION

(2) Inner Game Blueprint: Your One Habit That Dissolves Your Problems

Objective: Breaking a habit can seem like an insurmountable challenge, one that many of us struggle with.

This intervention will give you absolute clarity on the negative effects caused by the habit you want to break.

It's not an easy journey, but with a clear understanding of what's at stake, you will develop the willpower and discipline to start chipping away at breaking your one habit.

Step 1: Write down the habit you're trying to break. This simple act can help you become more aware of the habit and start taking steps to change it.

Step 2: Identify all the problems, issues, and pain points that this habit causes. This step requires introspection and honesty about the negative effects of the habit. It could be anything from health problems to financial difficulties to strained relationships.

Step 3: Assess the impact of each of these problems on your life and the lives of those around you. For example, in my case, my alcohol habit resulted in my poor performance in my career/ business; moreover, it had a negative impact on my self-esteem.

Step 4: This step will be taking the previous step further by quantifying the impact. Write down the cost of the habit to you, including your career/business. This could include the cost of medical treatment, lost productivity, or missed opportunities. Understanding the true cost of the habit will intensify your discipline and willpower to make a change.

Congratulations! By carrying out these steps, you have created an open loop in your mind. This loop is the awareness of the habit you're trying to break, and awareness of its negative impact on your life and on the people around you.

CHAPTER 4

THE ROAD TO RECOVERY

Journey of Triumph Over Adversity

BRING IT ON

THE CRUCIBLE OF ADVERSITY

Ah, adversity! The mischievous troublemaker that loves to throw obstacles our way, testing our strength, character, and resilience. It's like a crash course in personal growth, with a side of frustration and a sprinkle of hair-pulling moments.

When we find ourselves face-to-face with adversity, it's only natural to feel a whirlwind of emotions. We might want to unleash our inner Hulk, and shout at the unfairness of it all.

But here's the thing: Adversity is like that sneaky prankster who plays tricks on everyone, but each person reacts differently. We all have our own unique dance with adversity, and that's what makes life so intriguing.

In this chapter, we're going to dive headfirst into the wild world of adversity. We'll unravel its mysteries and explore how it can actually be the secret sauce for personal growth.

All of us have and will face adversity in our lives. It's like a rite of passage we go through as humans. Together, we'll navigate the stormy seas, ready to conquer whatever life throws our way.

Let the adventure begin!

FROM SILICON VALLEY TO DUBAI: A TRANSFORMING JOURNEY

Once upon a time, in the land of consulting and corporate ladders, I was a young go-getter, climbing my way to the top with determination and a pocket full of dreams. But deep down, there was a persistent itch, an entrepreneurial bug that refused to be ignored.

You see, my dad was like the mythical $100 bill in your back pocket—always chasing new ventures and embracing the world of entrepreneurship. Watching him weave his magic planted a seed in my heart, a seed that whispered, "Build something of your own, buddy!"

And so, with a combination of ambition and naivety, I decided to take the leap. I bid farewell to the cozy comforts of Silicon Valley and teamed up with my partner-in-crime, Avinash. Our destination? The dazzling desert oasis of Dubai.

Now, starting a business in a foreign land is no walk in the park. We encountered challenges that could make a seasoned entrepreneur quiver in their boots.

First on the list: cultural acrobatics. Dubai, with its melting pot of cultures, left us scratching our heads. But hey, we embraced the confusion and embarked on a crash course in cultural anthropology. Who knew building bridges across cultures could be both enlightening and hilarious?

But wait, there's more! The second challenge on our path to greatness was building a network from scratch. Picture us as networking novices, armed with business cards and enthusiasm, with a hint of desperation. We attended more networking events than we could count, shaking hands, making connections, and hoping that someone would give us a shot. It was like speed dating—but instead of finding love, we were hunting for business opportunities.

It took us years of sweat, perseverance, and the occasional bout of uncontrollable laughter, but we did it.

We conquered those challenges like bosses, built a thriving business, and helped countless companies in Dubai transform their IT systems and reach for the stars. Our hard work even earned us the title of one of the industry's fastest-growing companies.

THE ABYSS OF GRIEF

Two years after we moved to Dubai, my father-in-law passed away suddenly. It was a massive shock for all of us. I remember the look on my wife Jasmine's face when I told her that her father had passed away. It was the most difficult thing I've ever had to do in my life.

We were all devastated; however, over time, we began to heal. Our spiritual practice helped strengthen our resolve that, although Jasmine's father was no longer with us, his soul lives on.

LOYALTY IN THE FACE OF ADVERSITY

When my father-in-law passed away, my mother-in-law stepped up to take over the company. I knew that I had to do whatever I could to support her, so I stepped back from my role at Latitude Systems. My partner, Avi, was supportive and agreed to take on more responsibility at the company. I felt like a juggler precariously balancing flaming swords while riding a unicycle, but I knew that I had to try to help my mother-in-law and keep the company afloat.

As I was going through that difficult phase of finding alignment between my roles, I was filled with overwhelming joy when I learned that Jasmine and I were expecting a child.

GROWING OUR FAMILY: EMBRACING PARENTHOOD WITH ANTICIPATION

The news of our impending parenthood filled us with overwhelming joy. We made a conscious effort to dedicate time and energy to prepare for the arrival of our little one. We chose to keep the gender a surprise, eagerly embracing the thrill of the unknown.

As the due date drew closer, everything seemed to be going according to plan. We eagerly counted down the days and meticulously set up the nursery. However, life had a different script in store for us.

THE POWER OF INTUITION

I learned the hard way that ignoring my intuition can lead to problems. I ignored my gut feeling about a significant business decision, and it led to unforeseen challenges and setbacks.

Since then, I've learned that intuition is not a mystical force, but a culmination of my experiences, knowledge, and instincts. It's the wisdom of countless moments, successes, and failures distilled into subtle signals that we must learn to recognize and honor.

Embracing intuition requires courage and trust. It often defies the logic and reasoning we rely on so heavily. It calls us to embrace the realm of the unknown, to navigate uncharted territories with a blend of confidence and humility.

Through the lessons I've learned, I've discovered that intuition can be a formidable ally. It has led me to paths I may have overlooked or underestimated, helped me make better decisions, and enriched my life.

THE CALL

I received a call from a client urging me to travel to London. This caught me off guard, as my wife was due to give birth in three weeks. I was conflicted between my family and my career, but I knew that I had to seize this opportunity.

However, my mind was a battleground. One voice seductively whispered, "You can handle it all. Don't miss this chance for growth and success."

Meanwhile, another voice roared with undeniable truth, reminding me, "What about your priorities? Your family should always come first, no matter the allure of money or achievement."

The dueling voices within me fueled a sense of internal chaos. I was confused, anxious, and ultimately torn between my personal and professional responsibilities.

However, amidst the turmoil, I couldn't ignore the nagging feeling in my gut. Deep down, I knew what it was trying to tell me. I yearned to be there for my wife, to witness the miracle of our child's birth, and to provide the support that only a husband and father could.

DEPARTURE AND DOUBT

I boarded the plane to London, my heart heavy. I knew I was making a mistake, but I couldn't bring myself to stay home. I had to seize this opportunity.

As I sat in my seat, I thought about what I was missing. I imagined Jasmine in labor, our child's first cry, the moment I would finally meet them. Guilt washed over me, but I knew I had to stay focused.

- What am I missing by not being there for Jasmine?

- What will it be like to hear about the birth of my child secondhand?

- Will I ever forgive myself for missing this moment?

- What if something goes wrong?

- Will I regret this for the rest of my life?

I arrived in London late at night. I was exhausted, but I couldn't sleep. All I could think about was getting back on time.

- How am I going to live with myself?

- How am I going to look at Jasmine in the eye?

- How am I going to face my child?

I tried to push these thoughts aside, but they kept coming back. I felt guilty and anxious, and I couldn't shake the feeling that I was making a colossal mistake.

THE WEIGHT OF DISTANCE

In London, my heart was heavy. I tried to focus on my work, but I couldn't shake the feeling of guilt.

Finally, all my meetings were behind me. I was exhausted, but I was also relieved. I could finally relax and focus on getting back home.

THE CALL THAT CHANGED EVERYTHING

As I was about to pack my bags for the return flight, my phone rang. It was Jasmine, her voice trembling with urgency. She uttered the words that shattered my heart: "My water broke."

I was flooded with panic and regret as I grappled with the reality that I was thousands of kilometers away from Jasmine.

THE MIRACLE I DIDN'T SEE

I listened helplessly on the phone as my son was born. I could hear the chaos of the delivery room, the doctor's encouraging shouts, and Jasmine's grunts of effort. The news of "it's a boy!" pierced through me, evoking tears of both joy and anguish. I was so happy that my son was healthy, but I was also filled with regret that I had missed his birth.

I hung up the phone and sank to the floor, tears streaming down my face.

THE GUILT OF ABSENCE

The flight back felt like an eternity. I stared out the window, feeling the weight of my absence.

I thought about how I had left Jasmine alone to go on a business trip, and how I had missed the birth of my son. I felt ashamed.

Finally, the plane landed. I rushed to the hospital; I held them both.

THE GIFT OF SECOND CHANCES

I arrived at the hospital, anxious and remorseful. I knew that I had let Jasmine down, but I was also grateful to be there for her now.

I took a deep breath and spoke.

"I'm so sorry," I said. "I know that I let you down. I should have been here for you."

"I know," she said. "But I'm also so grateful that you're here now."

THE PRICE OF SUCCESS

I faced the consequences of my actions, wracked with regret. I had neglected my intuition, and now I was left to deal with the aftermath.

The damage was done. Holding my newborn baby in my hands, I knew that the consequences would continue to affect me. But amidst the darkness, a glimmer of hope emerged as I made a firm commitment to be the best father I could be.

I realized that I had measured success solely based on external factors, neglecting my inner voice. Prioritizing achievements, status, and material wealth led me astray from my true purpose and passions.

Prior to missing the birth of my son, I had slipped into the habit of ignoring my intuition. I became immune to its influence, growing broken on the inside. Outwardly, I maintained a facade of success, but internally, the lights had dimmed.

But now, I was finally ready to listen to my intuition. I was ready to commit to being the best father I could be. I was ready to redeem myself.

THE WAKE-UP CALL

I had been hit by a crisis that made me realize I had lost sight of the bigger picture. I had been so focused on my work that I had neglected my family. This wake-up call forced me to reevaluate my priorities and regain focus on what was truly important to me.

MALADAPTIVE COPING MECHANISMS

I thought I was good at coping with stress, but I now realize that my coping mechanisms were actually making my problems worse. I used three main maladaptive coping mechanisms: distraction, self-punishment, and avoidance.

THE DANGERS OF MALADAPTIVE COPING (AND HOW TO COPE BETTER)

Maladaptive coping mechanisms can lead to isolation, loneliness, overwhelm, and difficulty dealing with emotions in a healthy way. In the long run, they can make our problems worse.

I'm still learning how to cope in a healthy way. I'm learning to recognize and deal with maladaptive coping mechanisms in a healthier way. I'm learning to gain perspective and embrace the bigger picture. This helps me cope with the challenges of life and make better decisions.

THE FORK IN THE ROAD

I had reached a critical juncture in my life. My maladaptive coping mechanisms had taken their toll on my family, my business, and my health. I had to make a choice: Continue down the path of self-destruction or make a change. I chose to make a change.

I bought out Avi's share, and assembled a team to run the business in my place. I knew I needed to prioritize my physical and mental health, make lifestyle changes, and address the accumulated shame and regret within me. I also knew that I needed to have a clear vision for my future.

I had worked with an Neuro-linguistic Programming coach a few years ago who helped me to shape my future vision. This experience empowered me to create a powerful model of what I wanted to achieve, solidify my aspirations, and gain a profound sense of self. I knew that I needed to reclaim my vision and use it to guide me on my journey to recovery.

CONCLUSION

Adversity is a part of life. It is something that we will all face at some point. However, it is important to remember that adversity is not the end of the story—it's the beginning.

As Nelson Mandela once said, "The greatest glory in living lies not in never falling, but in rising every time we fall." This quote is a reminder that we should not be afraid of failure. Instead, we should learn from our mistakes and use them as an opportunity to grow stronger.

If we can learn from our mistakes and overcome our challenges, we will emerge stronger and more resilient. We will be better equipped to face whatever challenges life throws our way.

⅏⅏ INTERVENTION
The Inner Game Blueprint

Vision—your chance to craft your compelling future narrative.

What do you want right now?

_____

_____

Why do you want it?

_____

_____

Where are you right now?

_____

_____

When you have what you want, what will you see, hear, and feel?

_____

_____

How will you know when you have it?

_____

_____

What will you gain from this outcome, or what will it allow you to do?

_____

_____

Who will benefit and how?

_____

_____

What do you already have to be able to achieve it now, and what do you still need to achieve it?

_____

_____

What will happen if you don't get it?

_____

_____

CHAPTER 5

FROM DARKNESS
TO LIGHT

BRING
IT
ON

MY INNER GAME WAS CRUMBLING

Picture this: I was a successful entrepreneur, but my personal life was in chaos. My health was suffering. Then, my second son, Mikhayl was born, and I had an epiphany. I realized that I had been neglecting my family and my own well-being.

It was a classic case of "winning at business, failing at life".

You know that feeling when you've got it all, but deep down, you feel like you've misplaced something important, like your car keys or your sanity? That was me. I was on a roll, making decisions like a blindfolded dart-thrower, and the results were as predictable as a cat herding competition.

Sometimes you have to hit rock bottom to realize that you're digging in the wrong direction. And rock bottom can be quite a bumpy ride, like being on a rollercoaster with a broken track. But it's also a wake-up call, a chance to gather the shattered pieces of your life and start putting them back together, one puzzle piece at a time.

So, fasten your seatbelt and get ready for the rollercoaster ride of my life, where success and chaos collide. It's a tale of learning from my mistakes, finding balance, and discovering that true fulfillment goes beyond dollar signs and business triumphs.

Get ready for a wild ride.

This is the year that changed everything.

MY DARK NIGHT OF THE SOUL

I was successful in my career and had a beautiful family, but I was deeply unhappy. I felt like I was living a lie, and that I was not living up to my purpose and my full potential. I started to question everything I believed in, and I felt like I was losing my grip on reality.

I was in a fog. I couldn't think straight, and I didn't know what was real and what wasn't. I didn't know what was happening to me. I was scared and confused.

However, I realized that I needed to make a change. I was tired of feeling sick and tired.

THE SYMPTOMS

As a result, I started to experience all sorts of strange symptoms. I lost interest in the things I used to enjoy, like reading, spending time with my family and friends, or going for walks in nature. I felt weak and tired all the time, and I had trouble sleeping. I even lost 12kg in two months. My energy levels were really low, and I felt like my body was attacking itself.

The best way to describe it would be to imagine there's a fire inside your body.

I went to several doctors, but they couldn't find anything wrong with me physically. They said it was probably stress or anxiety, but

I knew it was something more. I was feeling lost and alone, and I didn't know what to do.

THE CONNECTION

I started to do some research, and I learned about the concept of "dark nights of the soul." A dark night of the soul is a period of intense spiritual and emotional turmoil. It's a time when our old beliefs and attachments are stripped away, leaving us feeling lost and alone. But it's also a time of great transformation. If we can persevere through this difficult period, we emerge stronger and more connected to our true selves.

I realized that I was going through a dark night of the soul. I was being forced to confront my deepest fears and insecurities. But I also knew that this was an opportunity for growth. I was determined to come out the other side stronger and more whole.

THE TRANSITION

The symptoms I experienced during this time were a physical manifestation of my inner turmoil. I was literally feeling the effects of my soul being stripped away. It was a painful and confusing time, but it was also a time of great transformation. I emerged from the other side stronger and more connected to my true self.

THE MENTAL SURGERY

I delved into countless motivational guides, articles, and books on working smarter, not harder, searching for a way to climb out of the deep hole I found myself in. They failed to address the underlying roots that were causing my issues to persist.

However, I realized that I needed a more invasive approach to change—a form of mental surgery that would address the deep-seated negative patterns of thinking that kept me stuck in a loop of despair. Simply reading books or articles promising a quick fix would only provide temporary relief, like painting over rust on an old car. The rust would inevitably resurface and spread.

THE RISK

I knew that if I didn't find a sustainable solution, I risked losing everything—and I mean everything. I was at a crossroads in my life. I could either continue down the same path and eventually destroy myself, or I could take a leap of faith and try something new.

However, I was afraid of what that might mean. I had always been a person who went after goals, but my inner dialogue was holding me back. I was afraid of failure, afraid of rejection, afraid of being seen as weak. But I knew that if I didn't take a chance, I would regret it for the rest of my life.

THE POWER OF INNER DIALOGUE

I'm always setting goals for myself, and I'm always looking for ways to achieve them. I'm not afraid to take risks, and I'm always willing to put in the hard work.

But sometimes, my inner dialogue can get in the way. I'll start to think about all the things that could go wrong, and I'll start to doubt myself. This can lead to anxiety and stress, making it difficult to focus on my goals.

Looking back at a snapshot of myself from this time, I am filled with a sense of shame. I was so preoccupied with running towards my goals that I never took the time to reflect on my well-being. Had I looked in the mirror, I would have seen the state I was in. My eyes were surrounded by dark, wrinkled rings, and my skin appeared pasty and sallow. My confidence was fleeting.

MUTING NEGATIVITY

I've always struggled with negative self-talk. I would constantly tell myself that I didn't deserve love, that there was never enough time, that I wasn't doing enough, that I needed to do more, and that I wasn't good enough. These negative thoughts had an over-whelming consequence on my life. They made me feel anxious, depressed, and isolated. They also made it difficult for me to achieve my goals.

THE THOUGHTS THAT HOLD US BACK

Maybe it's self-talk like "I'm not good enough" or "I'll never be successful". These words create a cascade of thoughts, which have a direct impact on our self-esteem, our motivation, and our ability to achieve our goals.

I know this from personal experience. In my twenties, I was afraid to speak up in meetings, ask for a promotion, or even try new things. I was constantly comparing myself to others, and feeling like I wasn't good enough.

One day, I had a wake-up call. I realized that I was letting these negative thoughts control my life. I was tired of feeling like I wasn't good enough. I wanted to live my life to the fullest, and I knew that I couldn't do that if I was constantly holding myself back.

So, I decided to challenge those thoughts. I made a conscious effort to focus on my strengths, such as my creativity and my ability to connect with people. I also stopped comparing myself to others and started to celebrate my own accomplishments.

I learned that these negative thoughts were optional. I could choose to believe something different.

I started by identifying the thought. Where did it come from? Is it based on reality, or is it just a story that I was telling myself? Once I started challenging the thought, I started to focus on my strengths and accomplishments.

FINDING THE LIGHT SWITCH

I was feeling very low. I was drowning in negativity. But then, I found something that changed everything.

I was sitting in my room, feeling sorry for myself, when I noticed a light switch on the wall. I had never noticed it before, but for some reason, it caught my eye. I got up and flipped the switch, and the room was filled with light.

The light was so faint at first, I could barely see it. But as I opened the door to let fresh air in, it grew brighter and brighter. I understood that I had been living in the dark for too long, listening to the negative voices in my head.

I had been listening to those voices for so long, I had forgotten I had a choice. I could choose to believe their lies, or I could choose to believe in myself.

I chose to believe in myself. I flipped the switch again, and the room was plunged back into darkness. But I didn't mind. I knew that the light was still there, waiting for me to find it again.

I realized that the light switch was a metaphor for my inner dialogue. The negative voices in my head were like the darkness, and the light switch was like my ability to choose to believe in myself.

I realized that I had the power to control my own thoughts. I could choose to listen to the negative voices, or I could choose to listen to the voice of my own inner strength.

I chose to listen to the voice of my inner strength. I flipped the light switch back on, and the room was filled with light. I was finally free from the darkness.

THE CRAZY ROOMMATE

I've always had a negative inner voice. I call it my CRM, or Crazy Roommate. It's a nagging voice in the back of my head that's always there to criticize me. It tells me I'm not good enough, smart enough, or worthy enough. It tells me I'll never achieve my goals and that I'm better off giving up.

I've learned to challenge the CRM's negative thoughts. I ask myself if they're really true. And most of the time, they're not.

HOW TO CHALLENGE NEGATIVE THOUGHTS

If you're struggling with negative thoughts, here are a few tips on how to challenge them:

1. Identify the thought. What is the negative thought that you're having? Where did it come from?

2. Challenge the thought. Is the thought really true? Is there any evidence to support it?

3. Focus on the positive. What are your strengths and accomplishments? What are you grateful for?

4. Practice mindfulness. Pay attention to your thoughts and emotions without judgment.

5. Seek professional help. If you're struggling to challenge negative thoughts on your own, consider seeking professional help from a therapist or a coach.

MY DARK NIGHT OF THE SOUL

I've been through a dark night of the soul, my intention for sharing my story with you is in the hope that it will help you to understand what you might be going through, if you are experiencing something similar.

CHALLENGES

- I was an entrepreneur and a father, and I was struggling to balance my work and family life.

- I was feeling like I was failing at both, and I was starting to question my purpose in life.

- I felt isolated and alone, and I was ashamed to reach out for help.

For me, the dark night of the soul was a time of great pain and confusion. But it was also a time of great transformation. I learned a lot about myself and about life. I learned that I am stronger than I thought I was. I learned that I am capable of more than I ever imagined. And I learned that I am connected to something much bigger than myself.

HOW I EMERGED FROM THE DARK NIGHT OF THE SOUL

- I started to explore new ways of thinking and behaving. I learned about mindfulness and gratitude, and I started to take better care of my physical health.

- I talked to my family and friends about what I was going through. This helped me to feel less alone, and it gave me the support I needed to heal.

- I started to see a coach, which helped me to understand my challenges and to develop strategies for overcoming them.

- I started to take care of myself. I made sure to get enough sleep, eat healthy foods, and exercise regularly.

- I started to do some soul-searching. I asked myself some tough questions about my life, my values, and my purpose. I also started to explore new ways of living and being.

WHAT I LEARNED

- There is a difference between who I am and what I do. What I do is just that—what I do. It does not define the essence of me. I am a valuable and worthy person, regardless of my accomplishments or failures.

- The ongoing process of my transformation is sustainable. I am still on my journey, but I am making progress every day. I am learning and growing, and I am becoming the person I was meant to be.

- Meditation is one of the most powerful habits one can develop. It has helped me to connect with my inner wisdom and to find peace and clarity in the midst of chaos.

- Everything I went through contributed to my growth. I learned a lot about myself and about the world. I also learned how to be more resilient and how to overcome challenges.

- As a Transformation Coach, I learned how to assist entrepreneurs in achieving their goals by helping them to master their Inner Game and overcome their limiting beliefs.

I am still on my journey, but I am grateful for the progress I have made. I know that I will continue to learn and grow, and I am excited to see what the future holds.

Looking back, I have gained a deeper understanding of how I am wired and how my past experiences have influenced my present behavior. I have come to realize that unprocessed emotions and painful memories from the past have a significant impact on how I navigate the present.

I have been fortunate enough to have a sideline coach to help me manage my Inner Game, and I now have several more coaches to lean on. This journey of discovery and self-exploration has helped me recover from the unintentional abuse I inflicted on my mind, body, and spirit.

I used to feel these negative states and tried to avoid them. However, I have learned to embrace them and use them as an opportunity for growth. I have learned to decipher the messages they contain and make better decisions from reliable emotional feedback.

FAST-FORWARD TO THE FUTURE ...

Pain comes in different packages, from physical and emotional to mental anguish. It carries no health warning label for a very special reason. I've learned that enduring pain is an intense teacher that avoidance deprives us of. The only way to the other side is through.

RYAN HOLIDAY'S FAMOUS QUOTE

"The obstacle in the path becomes the path. Never forget, within every obstacle is an opportunity to improve our condition."

This quote emphasizes the idea that obstacles are not necessarily something to be feared or avoided, but rather can be seen as opportunities for growth and improvement. By embracing challenges and obstacles, we can develop resilience and find new paths forward in our lives.

"The only thing that separates you from living a great life is the Inner Game in your head."

— DHIREN HARCHANDANI

CONCLUSION

In this chapter, we explored the importance of the Inner Game in our lives. We saw how our thoughts and emotions can exert a profound influence on our success and happiness. We also learned that we are in control of our own I G and that we can choose to focus on the positive.

The only thing that separates you from living a great life is the I G in your head. The only thing that stands in our way is our own thoughts and emotions. If we can learn to manage our I G, we can live a great life.

INTERVENTION
Inner Game Blueprint

Here's the 5-why technique to dissolve self-doubt

In the past, I'd bury any self-doubt that would surface. Over time, I realized that the self-doubt that tormented me didn't come from the ether, or the radio: it came from my head.

And burying it or sweeping it under the proverbial rug only made it worse.

One technique when dealing with self-doubt is called "The 5 Whys." This technique involves asking yourself "why" five times in order to dig deeper into the root cause of your self-doubt.

Here's how it works:

1. Identify the self-doubt that you're feeling. For example, "I'm not good enough."

2. Ask yourself why you feel this way. For example, "Why do I feel like I'm not good enough?"

3. Answer the question, and then ask yourself "why" again. Repeat this process four more times. Each time, try to go deeper and uncover the underlying beliefs or assumptions that are contributing to your self-doubt.

4. By the fifth "why," you should have reached the root cause of your self-doubt. For example:

Here's an example of the process I went through:

- "I'm not good enough because I made a mistake at work."

- "Why do I feel like making a mistake means I'm not good enough?"

- "Because I think I should be perfect and never make mistakes."

- "Why do I think I need to be perfect?"

- "Because I don't want to disappoint others or be judged negatively."

- "Why do I care so much about what others think?"

Through this process of questioning, you may discover that your self-doubt is rooted in beliefs or assumptions that are not helpful or accurate.

By challenging these beliefs and assumptions, you can begin to shift your mindset and build more confidence in your Inner Game.

INTERVENTION

The Inner Game Blueprint: How Empowered Are You?

An essential item in the entrepreneur's toolkit is the bolster of empowerment. Unlike the builders' bolster used with a hammer to break bricks and mortar, bolstering entrepreneurial empowerment is a delicate process. And empowerment is top of the list involving getting to the bare bones of entrepreneurship.

But how do you get to bare-boned empowerment? Great question!

Deftly, like a surgeon separating ligament from bone, *you* divide what you *don't need* from what is *essential* for your survival and longevity. Entrepreneurship without empowerment is like a car without an engine, going nowhere fast.

Step 1:

ACTION
Make a list of What:

makes you happy?
fulfills you?
brings you contentment?

1. _____

2. _____

3. _____

4. _____

5. _____

6. _____

7. _____

8. _____

9. _____

10. _____

Step 2:

PAUSE
Look at your list again.

Step 3:

Place a (✓) next to the things that you control.

Place a (x) next to the things that are out of your control. (These things are dependent on people and place in your environment.)

Results

Empowerment = (✓)
Disempowerment = (x)

1. _____

2. _____

3. _____

4. _____

5. _____

6. _____

7. _____

8. _____

9. _____

10. _____

Conclusion:

More checks than crosses = EMPOWERED

More crosses than checks = LESS EMPOWERED

TAKING BACK CONTROL

Step 4:

Now answer this question for those you have marked with an (x): What do you need to change in order to take back control and not be dependent on anything outside of you?

1. _____

_____

_____

2. _____

_____

_____

3. _____

_____

_____

4. _____

_____

_____

5. _____

_____

_____

6. _____

_____

_____

7. _____

_____

_____

8. _____

_____

_____

REFLECTION

The less empowered you are, the more you are held back.

Empowerment comes from taking back control.

Knowing your state of empowerment from this brief exercise opens the trapdoor to the basement of hidden answers.

CHAPTER 6

FROM ROCK-BOTTOM
TO BRINGING IT ON

A Journey of Transformation and Self-Belief

BRING
IT
ON

"Self-belief is not negotiable."

— DHIREN HARCHANDANI

In the depths of my darkest soul-crushing moment, when it felt like the universe was playing a cruel joke on me, little did I know that it was actually setting the stage for an epic transformation.

I felt like the universe was giving me a wake-up call. I had been coasting through life, not really achieving my full potential. But then, something happened. I hit rock bottom. I was lost, confused, and scared. But it was also the beginning of my journey to success.

I learned a lot along the way. I learned that I am capable of more than I ever thought possible. I learned that I could overcome any challenge if I set my mind to it. And I learned that I have the power to make a difference in the world.

I'm not perfect, but I'm pretty great. I've achieved some amazing things, but I'm still hungry for more. I'm always looking for new challenges and new ways to make a difference.

After emerging from the depths of despair, I went on to achieve some things that were beyond my perceived limits.

- From a successful exit to coaching entrepreneurs whose businesses had a combined revenue of $2.5 Billion.

- I have completed over 2500 hours of coaching entrepreneurs, leaders, and organizations.

- I have also been recognized as one of the top 40 Changemakers in my industry.

- I have even completed ultra-races like the Ironman Triathlon.

Yes, I went from rock bottom to "bringing it on!"

I'm sharing this to show you what's possible when you find the light at the end of your own soul's dark tunnel.

I firmly believe that each and every one of us has the potential to achieve greatness, no matter how deep we've fallen. The key is to never give up on ourself, even when life is throwing punches like a boxer on steroids.

So, let my story be a reminder to you. A reminder that self-belief is non-negotiable.

THE IMPORTANCE OF SELF-BELIEF FOR ENTREPRENEURS

I've always been an entrepreneur at heart. I love the idea of starting my own business and building something from scratch. But I've also always struggled with self-doubt. I'm constantly second-guessing myself and wondering if I'm good enough.

Over the years, I've learned that self-belief is essential for success. It's what gives you the courage to take risks, the determination to overcome challenges, and the resilience to bounce back from setbacks.

I've seen firsthand how self-belief can help entrepreneurs achieve great things. I've met entrepreneurs who have overcome incredible odds to build successful businesses. And I've seen how self-belief can help entrepreneurs overcome their own fears and doubts.

So, if you're an entrepreneur, I encourage you to embrace your self-belief. It's the most important asset you have.

SELF-DOUBT: A POWERFUL MOTIVATOR

Self-doubt is a powerful motivator. It can be a dark cloud that hangs over your head, or it can be a fire in your belly that drives you to succeed.

I've experienced both sides of self-doubt. There have been times when I've let it paralyze me, and there have been times when I've used it as a source of motivation.

The key is to learn how to manage self-doubt. When it starts to creep in, acknowledge it, but don't let it control you. Challenge your negative thoughts and focus on your strengths.

Self-doubt can be a powerful tool, but it's important to use it wisely.

MANAGING SELF-DOUBT: TIPS FOR SUCCESS

- Acknowledge your self-doubt. The first step to managing it is to acknowledge that it exists.

- Challenge your self-doubt. Ask yourself if your negative thoughts are true and realistic.

- Focus on your strengths. Everyone has strengths and weaknesses. When you're feeling down, focus on your strengths to boost your confidence.

- Set realistic goals. Setting unrealistic goals can lead to self-doubt. Set goals that are achievable and will help you to build momentum.

BELIEF IN YOURSELF: EMBRACE A LITTLE DELUSION

One of the most important things you can do as an entrepreneur is to believe in yourself. Even if it's to the point of delusion.

This doesn't mean denying reality or acting arrogantly. It means having an unshakeable belief in your own abilities and potential.

Of course, you need to be realistic about your goals. But you also need to have a big enough dream that it scares you a little bit.

If you don't believe in yourself, no one else will. So, believe in yourself, even when it feels irrational.

THE IMPORTANCE OF SELF-BELIEF FOR ENTREPRENEURS: A PERSONAL PERSPECTIVE

I've been an entrepreneur for over 20 years. And I've learned a lot about the importance of self-belief along the way.

I've faced my fair share of challenges. There have been times when I've doubted myself, and times when I've wanted to give up. But I've always found a way to keep going.

And I know that I've only been able to do that because of my self-belief. I believe in myself, and I believe in my ability to achieve my goals.

I'm not saying that I've never had self-doubt. I have. But I've learned how to manage it. I've learned how to challenge my negative thoughts, and I've learned how to focus on my strengths.

Self-belief and essentialism are two key ingredients for a success-ful and fulfilling life.

When we combine self-belief with essentialism, we create a pow-erful force that can propel us toward our desired outcomes. We become unstoppable.

"Essentialism is the disciplined pursuit of less."

— GREG MCKEOWN, AUTHOR OF *ESSENTIALISM: THE DISCIPLINED PURSUIT OF LESS*

ESSENTIALISM: THE KEY TO A SIMPLER, MORE MEANINGFUL LIFE

During my dark night of the soul, I was drowning in chaos. My calendar was packed with back-to-back meetings, my to-do list seemed never-ending, and stress consumed me. I knew something had to change: I needed to reclaim my life.

That's when essentialism entered the scene. It was like a breath of fresh air in the midst of a suffocating storm. Essentialism taught me to focus on what truly mattered, to strip away the excess, and to live with intention and purpose. It became my guiding philosophy, transforming my life in profound ways.

Embracing essentialism wasn't easy. It meant confronting uncomfortable truths about myself and my choices. I had to let go of activities and commitments that were draining my energy and not aligned with my values. It was a process of shedding layers, and with each release, I felt a weight lifted off my shoulders.

As I started focusing on the essential few things, I discovered a newfound sense of relief and lightness. I had more time and energy to invest in the things that brought me joy and fulfillment: quality time with loved ones, pursuing my passions, and taking care of myself. I began to see the beauty in simplicity and found a deeper meaning in each moment.

One of the most powerful lessons essentialism taught me was the art of saying no. I used to be a people-pleaser, always saying yes to every request that came my way. But I realized that by saying yes to everything, I was saying no to myself. Learning to set boundaries and prioritize my own well-being became essential to living a more intentional life.

Essentialism goes beyond decluttering physical spaces—it's about decluttering our minds and hearts too. It's about evaluating our relationships, commitments, and even our own thoughts and beliefs. By consciously choosing what truly matters, we create space for what brings us joy and fulfillment.

Essentialism has been a game-changer for me. It's brought peace and simplicity to my once-chaotic existence. It's given me a roadmap to navigate the overwhelming demands of modern life with clarity and purpose.

FROM ASTHMA TO IRONMAN: AN ENTREPRENEUR'S JOURNEY THROUGH ENDURANCE SPORTS

Essentialism has also helped me in my journey as an endurance athlete. It has taught me the importance of focus and prioritization, and it has helped me to stay disciplined even when things get tough.

Let me take you back to my childhood when I battled with asthma, carrying an inhaler everywhere I went. Never in my wildest dreams could I have imagined that one day I would climb mountains and compete in Ironman races. The transformation from relying on an inhaler to becoming an Ironman was purely funded by self-belief and pushing my limits.

I can still vividly recall the days when even swimming 200 meters seemed like an insurmountable challenge, and running beyond three kilometers felt impossible. The idea of completing a full Ironman was beyond my comprehension.

As an entrepreneur and coach, I am often asked why cultivating self-belief is crucial for CEOs and entrepreneurs. The truth is, I have witnessed firsthand the remarkable influence self-belief has on business performance. It's not solely about having the right strategy or market forces; it's about nurturing the right mindset—the "Inner Game".

When entrepreneurs grasp the concept that their choices and decisions shape their reality, everything changes. They recognize that their mindset becomes the ultimate sustainable competitive advantage. By aligning their "Inner Game," they gain the clarity required to drive their businesses forward.

ENDURANCE SPORTS AND ENTREPRENEURSHIP: A TALE OF PARALLELS

In the realm of endurance sports, where athletes push their bodies to the limits, a fascinating parallel emerges with the world of entrepreneurship. It's a symbiotic relationship where valuable lessons from long-distance races seamlessly translate into the entrepreneurial journey, creating a powerful synergy.

Imagine starting with small strides, just like the initial challenge of swimming a mere 200 meters. In both endurance sports and entrepreneurship, progress is made by learning from mistakes, honing skills, and steadily advancing. It's a journey of ascending the ladder of endurance, pushing beyond comfort zones, and embracing the discomfort that comes with growth. As physical endurance strengthens, so does mental resilience, enabling the capacity to overcome obstacles and find innovative solutions.

Let's not overlook the moments of disappointment that inevitably arise. I recall the heartbreak I went through when I was training for over a year, for the longest Ultra (300 km) desert race in the world. I was devastated to receive news that it was being canceled two weeks before the race. This was a setback akin to a failed business deal. Yet, as entrepreneurs, we understand that setbacks cannot define us. We adapt, seek new opportunities, and continue our preparation with unwavering determination.

The profound lesson that both endurance sports and entrepreneurship teach us is that the ultimate competition lies within ourselves. It's not about comparing our achievements to others; it's about consistently surpassing our own limits. Both endeavors require embracing challenges, adapting to unforeseen circumstances, and making bold decisions even when things don't unfold as planned.

Engaging in endurance sports transcends the race itself; it becomes a transformative journey. The dedication, adaptability, and strategic planning involved contribute to becoming a better version of ourselves. Endurance sports shape us, instilling qualities that extend far beyond the racecourse.

As my coach Rob Foster often reminds me, "Endurance sports make you better at life!" This sentiment holds true in my personal journey from asthma to Ironman. It has honed my time management skills, refined my planning abilities, and fortified my determination to push beyond perceived limits. The lessons learned through endurance sports have undeniably made me a better entrepreneur: a more resilient, focused, and adaptable version of myself.

SOCIAL MEDIA: THE UNEXPECTED BUTTERFLY EFFECT

Social media is a realm of infinite possibilities. Who could have anticipated the extraordinary encounters that might stem from a simple Instagram post? Allow me to recount the fascinating tale of Neil, the man who slid into my DMs like a penguin on ice, igniting a chain reaction of events.

Several years ago, I decided to share a photo of myself holding the very last alcoholic beverage I would ever consume. Little did I know that Neil, a complete stranger at the time, would stumble upon this post and ignite a spark of curiosity. Neil had been grappling with his own battle against alcohol and was eager to learn how I achieved my triumph over the demon drink.

Intrigued by his desperation, I probed for more details. Neil had spent what felt like an eternity attempting to liberate himself from the clutches of alcohol but found himself continuously falling short. I saw myself in his struggle; I shared my journey with this stranger.

I began by posing a question that would make Socrates proud: "What decision could you make that would solve forty or fifty of your problems?" This question provoked deep contemplation within Neil, ultimately leading him to a brilliant realization: I was quitting alcohol.

However, the story takes an intriguing turn. Neil discovered that this seemingly unenjoyable habit served a purpose in his life. It provided him with a sense of belonging and acceptance among his drinking buddies, making him fear exclusion and cleverly crafted jests that attacked his masculinity.

But here's where the magic happens. As Neil began to peel back the layers of his boozy facade, he unearthed something extraordinary. By bidding farewell to alcohol, he restored his relationships with his loved ones and, more importantly, with himself. He discerned who his true friends were—those who didn't require booze to validate their bond. Astonishingly, Neil's commitment to sobriety even resulted in a promotion at work, as he now showed up punctually and excelled in his role (a revelation, indeed!).

And behold, the physical transformation was nothing short of remarkable. Neil joined a gym, shed unwanted pounds, and found himself noticing the beauty of autumn leaves strewn along the sidewalk. As it turns out, those leaves were not mere decorative debris after all!

But that's not all! This Instagram-sparked friendship between Neil and me set off a chain reaction. Another individual from the Entrepreneurs Organization witnessed the post and thought, "Hey, perhaps I should embark on a similar journey!" And just like that, I found myself coaching him through his own transformative process.

All of this, stemming from one seemingly inconsequential Instagram post. Who would have imagined it? The power of social media, my friends, is an untamed and unpredictable force. It possesses the ability to connect, inspire, and even change lives. So, the next time you find yourself mindlessly scrolling through your feed, remember that a tale of triumph might be waiting to leap out at you.

While my story is about alcohol, it's important to remember that the essence of my story is about habits that seem harmless on the surface, but can have a ripple effect on other areas of our lives. These habits can seem unrelated, but they are all connected. Overcoming these habits is like scaling Mount Everest: it's a difficult journey, but it's possible with the right support.

Here's to vulnerability, humor, and the unexpected butterfly effect of social media. May it continue to deliver positive consequences and alter lives in unimaginable ways.

TRANSFORMATION ARCHITECT: UNLEASHING POTENTIAL IN OTHERS

As a Transformation Coach, I work with ambitious and driven leaders who are constantly striving to reach new heights of performance. I believe that with the right coaching, transformation becomes an inevitable outcome.

My ultimate goal is to create optimal conditions for my clients to achieve their desired objectives. Together, we set goals in a way that ensures their realization in both their personal and professional lives. I wholeheartedly believe that with the right coaching, true transformation is not only possible but probable.

I am passionate about helping people reach their full potential, and I believe that everyone has the power to transform their lives. I am honored to be a part of that journey, and I look forward to helping others unleash their inner power.

AS A CONSCIOUS LEADER

I used to be a driven and ambitious entrepreneur. At the same time, I was stressed, anxious, and unfulfilled. I realized that I needed to make a change, so I embarked on a journey of self-discovery and personal transformation.

I learned that the key to sustainable success is to master your Inner Game. This means aligning your mindset, emotions, and body so that you can navigate challenges with clarity and resilience. It also means prioritizing your well-being and nurturing meaningful relationships.

As a conscious leader, I've learned that success is about more than achieving external milestones. It is also about embodying a holistic approach that honors your humanity and the well-being of those around you.

I am passionate about guiding leaders towards reaching their full potential and creating a positive impact on the world.

AS A KEYNOTE SPEAKER: EMPOWERING AND INSPIRING THROUGH AUTHENTICITY

I used to be terrified of public speaking. Yet, I knew I had something valuable to share, so I faced my fear head-on. With practice, patience, and persistence, I learned to harness my nervous energy and transform it into an electrifying presence on stage.

Today, I step onto the stage with a surge of adrenaline and a deep sense of purpose. I thrive on the genuine connection I establish with the audience, knowing that my words have the power to inspire, motivate, and transform lives.

If you find yourself grappling with the fear of public speaking, I want you to know that you are not alone. With dedication and perseverance, anyone can overcome this fear and discover the exhilaration of finding your voice. Embrace the journey, and remember that the best way to conquer fear is by bringing it on.

CONCLUSION

In conclusion, self-belief and essentialism are vital qualities for entrepreneurs. Focusing on what truly matters, everything else becomes a distraction.

I want to leave you with a quote that I find relatable and that sums up the chapter's message:

"The difference between a successful person and others is not a lack of strength, not a lack of knowledge, but rather a lack of will."

— VINCE LOMBARDI

INTERVENTION

Inner Game Blueprint: Self-doubt Detox

How often is this happening?

_____

_____

What am I doubting?

_____

_____

Where does it come from? (very important!)

_____

_____

Is it true?

_____

_____

What do I need to do to overcome this feeling of self-doubt?

_____

_____

Self-doubt deserves its own book, so please don't think this short section is the definitive answer to everything surrounding the topic. Having said that, it is essential to note that there is a close resemblance, not to be confused, between self-doubt and measured caution.

As I reflect back on my twenties, and through my coaching of leaders, I've come to learn that one of the biggest obstacles is self-doubt. For me, my main thought in my twenties was: 'I'm not good enough'. It was subconscious; I wasn't even aware that it was there.

Consciously I wasn't trying to outperform it, I was trying to outrun it. Had I known that it's just a thought, and all thoughts are optional, I would have picked a more empowering sentence, like "I'm unstoppable" or "I'm fearless".

The words were creating my reality, which is why we have to be very specific with the language that we use in the privacy of our mind—it only creates a reality.

CHAPTER 7

THE DISCIPLINE OF CONSISTENCY

BRING
IT
ON

"Discipline, not ideas, is the key to real success."

— CHET HOLMES

Are you tired of feeling like a champion for a hot minute, only to sputter out like a deflated balloon? If so, you're not alone. The secret sauce to achieving your goals is consistency.

Motivation is a fickle friend, who shows up fashionably late and leaves without a trace. Discipline, on the other hand, is the superhero cape that keeps us on track, even when life throws flaming hurdles our way.

In this chapter, we'll unravel the mysteries of consistency and its unrivaled power in the realm of success.

We'll dissect motivation and discipline, showing you why the latter is the real MVP (most valuable player) for long-term triumph.

So, get cozy, grab some popcorn (or kale chips, if you're feeling fancy), and prepare to embrace the consistency revolution.

Let's bring it on!

MOTIVATION vs. DISCIPLINE

Motivation is like a spark. It can get us started on a task, but it doesn't always last. Discipline, on the other hand, is like fire. It's what keeps us going even when we're tired or discouraged.

Motivation is often fueled by external factors, such as the desire to win a competition or get a promotion. Discipline, on the other hand, is more internal. It's the ability to do what we need to do, even when we don't feel like it.

So, which is more important: motivation or discipline?

The truth is, both are important. But if I had to choose one, I would say that discipline is more important. Because even if we have the motivation to start a task, without discipline we're likely to give up when things get tough.

Discipline is what will help us to stay on track and achieve our goals, even when motivation is lacking.

SELF-DOUBT CRUSHED ME, BUT DISCIPLINE HELPED ME EMERGE VICTORIOUS

I had always been a driven and motivated person. I set goals for myself and worked hard to achieve them. But there was one area of my life where I struggled: my Inner Game.

My Inner Game is the mental and emotional state that I bring to my athletic and professional endeavors. It's the difference between giving up when things get tough, and pushing through to victory.

For years, I struggled with self-doubt. I would start a project or a workout program with great enthusiasm, and then I would quickly lose motivation. I would tell myself that I wasn't good enough or that I wasn't capable of achieving my goals.

But then, something changed. I started to realize that motivation wasn't enough. I needed discipline.

With discipline, I was able to overcome my self-doubt and achieve my goals. I started training harder and eating healthier. I became more focused and determined.

I'm not saying that discipline is easy. It's not. But it's worth it. Discipline is what will help you achieve your goals, no matter how difficult they may seem.

FUN FACT

The importance of discipline can be proved mathematically by adding the incremental value of the letters of the alphabet. Starting with A=1 and ending on Z=26, the total value of the letters in the word "discipline" is 100%.

This is a reminder that discipline is essential for success. It's what will help you achieve your goals, no matter how difficult they may seem.

D+I+S+C+I+P+L+I+N+E = 100%

HOW DISCIPLINE HAS HELPED PEOPLE ACHIEVE THEIR GOALS

Discipline is the secret ingredient for success in any area of life. Whether it's shedding those extra pounds, snagging that coveted promotion, or starting your own flourishing business, discipline is the guiding light that paves the way.

Research shows that disciplined individuals are more likely to shed pounds and maintain their weight loss, compared to their undisciplined counterparts. And in the realm of careers, disciplined employees have a higher chance of climbing up that corporate ladder.

Now, let's dive into the diverse ways people develop discipline. Some swear by setting goals and crafting meticulous plans. Others find solace in tracking progress and rewarding themselves for each milestone. And let's not forget the power of a supportive tribe—finding like-minded folks who can keep the motivational fire burning.

HOW DO YOU GAUGE CONSISTENT SUCCESS?

The Yo-Yo method? Not the way to go. It's like riding a roller coaster, where you're up one day and down the next. Talk about a demoralizing joyride that drains your motivation.

Instead, let's focus on what truly matters: the aspects of success within your control. We're talking about discipline, sincerity, and integrity, the holy trinity of achievement. When you possess these qualities, you'll radiate pride, no matter what day it is.

Discipline gives you the strength to stick to your goals, even when you'd rather binge-watch your favorite series. Sincerity means being honest with yourself and others, keeping things real in this wacky journey of life. And let's not forget integrity, which is all about doing what you say you'll do, walking the talk like a boss.

These qualities are the sturdy foundation of consistent success. They may not have the glitz and glamour of a red-carpet event, but they'll be your faithful companions on the path to achieving your wildest dreams. So, buckle up, embrace discipline, wear sincerity like a crown, and let integrity be your guiding star.

LET ME REGALE YOU WITH A TALE STRAIGHT FROM THE COACHING ARCHIVES OF MY MENTOR ANAND RAO, THE MASTER OF TRANSFORMATION!

So, there's this client of his who dove headfirst into the world of habit change by devouring *Atomic Habits* by James Clear. It's like the Bible of behavior change, guiding folks on the path to remarkable results. Anand and his client had been discussing the mystical power of discipline. While reading the book, this client made a groundbreaking discovery: making his bed for three consecutive days!

Now, I know what you're thinking: making a bed sounds as mundane as watching paint dry. But for this client, it was nothing short of a cosmic shift. This brave soul had battled a lifetime of indiscipline, and conquering the bed-making mountain was a monumental triumph.

Here's the revelation: small changes in discipline have the audacity to produce massive results! It's like a magical potion that compounds over time, transforming the mundane into the extraordinary. If you're itching to achieve your goals, embrace the power of starting small. Because even the tiniest changes can ignite a wildfire of transformation.

What seem like minuscule adjustments in behavior hold the key to unlocking the doors of greatness. Who knows, maybe making your bed consistently will pave the way for conquering the world. It all starts with the small stuff. Embrace it, and let the magic unfold.

Here are some additional thoughts on how small changes can produce massive results

- The compound effect.
  - The compound effect is the idea that small, consistent changes can lead to big results over time. This is because the effects of our actions are cumulative.

- The snowball effect.
  - The snowball effect is a metaphor for how small changes can grow into something much larger. This is because small

changes can create momentum, which can lead to even bigger changes.

Discipline is the foundation of consistency. It's the ability to do what needs to be done, even when you don't feel like it. It's the ability to stay focused on your goals, even when things get tough.

When you're disciplined, you're more likely to be consistent. You're more likely to stick to your plans and habits, even when they're not easy. You're more likely to reach your goals, no matter how big or small.

So, if you want to be more consistent, start by building discipline.

Here are a few tips:

- Set small, achievable goals. This will make it easier to stay motivated and on track.

- Break down large goals into smaller, more manageable steps. This will make them seem less daunting and more attainable.

- Reward yourself for your accomplishments. When you reach a milestone, take some time to celebrate your success. This will help you stay motivated and on track.

- Find an accountability partner. This can be a friend, family member, or coach who can help you stay on track.

- Find a support system. Having people who believe in you and support your goals can make a big difference.

- Eliminate distractions. When you're trying to be disciplined, it's important to eliminate distractions. This means turning off your phone, closing your email, and finding a quiet place to work.

- Create a routine and stick to it. This will help you stay on track and make it easier to be consistent.

Remember, discipline is not about being perfect. It's about doing the right things, even when you don't feel like it. If you can be disciplined, you'll be well on your way to achieving your goals.

THE IMPORTANCE OF CONSISTENCY

Consistency is one of the most important keys to unlock success. When you're consistent, you're more likely to achieve your goals and reach your full potential. There are many benefits to consistency, including:

- Building better habits
- Achieving your goals
- Improving your self-confidence

Consistency is not easy, but it is possible with the help of metacognition.

METACOGNITION AND DISCIPLINE

Metacognition is the ability to think about your own thoughts. It is the process of becoming aware of your own thoughts and how they are affecting you. This can be a powerful tool for discipline, as it allows you to identify and challenge negative thoughts that are holding you back.

For example, let's say you are trying to lose weight. You may have a negative thought that says, "I'm not good enough to lose weight." This thought can lead to feelings of discouragement and hopelessness, which can make it difficult to stick to your diet and exercise plan. However, if you are aware of this thought, you can challenge it by saying something like, "That's not true. I am capable of losing weight, and I am going to do it."

Metacognition can also help you to stay focused on your goals. When you are aware of your thoughts, you can identify any distractions that are getting in your way. For example, if you're preparing for an interview, you may have a thought that says, "I'm bored." This thought can lead to you checking your phone or going on social media. However, if you are aware of this thought, you can challenge it by saying something like, "I'm not bored. I'm just feeling a little restless. I'm going to take a short break and then get back to preparing."

HOW TO PRACTICE METACOGNITION

There are many ways to practice metacognition. Here are a few ideas:

- Journaling: Keep a journal of your thoughts and feelings. This can help you to become more aware of your inner dialogue.

- Meditation: Meditation is a great way to focus your attention on the present moment and to become aware of your thoughts and feelings.

- Mindfulness exercises: There are many mindfulness exercises that can help you to develop metacognition. One simple exercise is to focus on your breath for a few minutes. Notice the sensations of your breath as it enters and leaves your body.

By becoming aware of your thoughts and how they are affecting you, you can challenge negative thoughts and stay focused on your goals. There are many ways to practice metacognition, so find a method that works for you and start practicing today.

CONCLUSION

Discipline is the key to achieving our goals. It is about being consistent and focused, even when things get tough. We can use metacognition to our advantage by becoming aware of our own thoughts, and challenging negative thoughts that are holding us back. The reality is that everything starts with a thought, like the lightbulb, the airplane, and even the idea of discipline itself.

"Discipline is the bridge between goals and accomplishment."

— JIM ROHN

EISENHOWER MATRIX

	URGENT	NOT URGENT
IMPORTANT	**STRENGTHS** ✓ Do it now.	**DECIDE** Schedule a time to do it.
NOT IMPORTANT	**DELEGATE** Who can do it for you?	**DELETE** Eliminate it.

TOOL
The Eisenhower Matrix

The Eisenhower Matrix is a simple but effective tool that can help you prioritize your tasks. It was created by Dwight D. Eisenhower, the 34th President of the United States.

THE DISCIPLINE OF CONSISTENCY

Using the Eisenhower Matrix to Stay Consistent

The Eisenhower Matrix is a great tool for helping you stay consistent with your goals. By using the Eisenhower Matrix, you can focus on the tasks that are most important and urgent, and you can avoid wasting time on tasks that are not important or urgent. This will help you stay on track with your goals and achieve them more quickly.

Here are the steps on how to use the Eisenhower Matrix to stay consistent

1. List all of your tasks. This includes both the tasks that you need to do and the tasks that you want to do.

2. Categorize each task into one of the four quadrants.

3. Prioritize your tasks. Focus on the tasks in the "Important and urgent" quadrant first.

4. Schedule your tasks. Schedule the tasks in the "Important but not urgent" quadrant for later.

5. Delegate or ignore the tasks in the "Not important but urgent" quadrant.

6. Ignore or delegate the tasks in the "Not important and not urgent" quadrant.

By following these steps, you can use the Eisenhower Matrix to stay consistent with your goals and achieve them more quickly.

Here are some examples of tasks that would fall into each quadrant:

- Important and urgent: Meeting a deadline, responding to an urgent email, fixing a broken computer

- Important but not urgent: Planning a vacation, writing a blog post, working on a long-term project

- Not important but urgent: Answering a non-urgent email, attending a meeting that you don't need to be at, running an errand

- Not important and not urgent: Watching TV, browsing social media, playing video games

The Eisenhower Matrix is a simple but effective tool that can help you be more productive and efficient. By using the tool, you can focus on the tasks that are most important and urgent, and you can avoid wasting time on tasks that are not important or urgent.

The Eisenhower Matrix has many benefits, including:

- Helping you prioritize your tasks. The Eisenhower Matrix can help you focus on the tasks that are most important and urgent.

- Increasing your productivity. By focusing on the most important tasks, you can be more productive and get more done in less time.

- Reduces stress. When you know what you need to do and when you need to do it, you can feel more in control and less stressed.

The Eisenhower Matrix is a simple but effective tool that can help you be more productive and efficient.

CHAPTER 8

THE COMPARISON TRAP

How to Break Free from the
Endless Cycle of Self-doubt

BRING
IT
ON

THE PUBLIC SPEAKING CURSE

I used to believe that public speaking was my kryptonite. It all started back in school when I had to deliver a few lines in a play and the audience burst into laughter. Talk about a confidence killer! From then on, I was convinced I was terrible at public speaking, and I avoided it like the plague.

One day, it hit me like a bolt of lightning: I realized my friends and teachers were dead wrong. It's not that I was bad at public speaking; I just needed to rebuild my confidence.

So, I rolled up my sleeves and started practicing. I gave presentations to my friends and family, who were kind enough to endure my nervous rambling.

That was tough. It wasn't a walk in the park, but I kept at it, practicing and practicing until I started to see progress (more on this later).

This whole experience taught me a valuable lesson about the power of conditioning. We may be conditioned to believe certain things about ourselves, but guess what? It's not set in stone. We can liberate ourselves from those limiting beliefs and create a whole new reality.

This chapter is all about how I shifted my perceived reality. I hope that by sharing my story, you'll be inspired to do the same. It's not always easy, but it's possible. And it can have a profound effect on your life.

Let's dive in!

HOW IS REALITY CREATED?

Our reality is created by the interaction of our senses, conditioning, and behavior. Our senses allow us to perceive the world around us, while our conditioning shapes how we interpret our experiences. Our behavior is the driving force behind the results we achieve in life.

OUR CONDITIONING

Our conditioning is the sum total of our thoughts, beliefs, values, and experiences. It's like a pair of tinted glasses that influences how we view and interpret the world. For example, if we were raised in a family that believed that public speaking was a terrifying experience, we would be more likely to have a negative view of public speaking ourselves.

OUR SENSES

Our senses allow us to perceive the world around us through sight, sound, smell, taste, and touch. However, our senses are not perfect. They can be influenced by our conditioning, our expectations, and our emotions. For example, if we are afraid of spiders, we might see a harmless spider as a giant, hairy monster.

OUR BEHAVIOR

Our behavior is the culmination of all our thoughts and actions. It's the dance between our intentions and our actions, as we navigate through the tapestry of our conditioning and interact with the world around us. Our behavior holds the key to manifesting the reality we desire. For example, if we want to be more confident public speakers, we need to practice public speaking and challenge our negative beliefs about public speaking.

A PERSONAL EXAMPLE

I used to believe that I was a terrible public speaker. I had a lot of negative beliefs about public speaking, such as "I'm not good enough" and "I'm going to make a fool of myself." These beliefs were shaped by my conditioning, which included a few bad experiences with public speaking in school.

However, I realized that my negative beliefs were holding me back. I wanted to be able to speak up and share my message with small and large groups, without feeling anxious or afraid.

So, I started to challenge my negative beliefs about public speaking. I started by giving small presentations to my friends and family. I signed up for a public speaking course that was transformative, where I got to practice speaking in front of a group of people.

It wasn't easy at first, but I kept practicing and, eventually, I started to feel more confident.

Then, the big moment arrived. I was asked to give a talk in front of 200 people. Cue the butterflies in my stomach, and all the fear from my past haunting me.

Still, deep down, I knew I had prepared. I took a deep breath, gave the talk, and you know what? It went shockingly well!

Gradually, things started to change. I began to feel more confident, and believe it or not, I actually started to enjoy public speaking. Who would have thought?

I'm not saying that I'm a natural public speaker, but I'm no longer afraid of it. I know that I can give a great talk, and I'll enjoy every second of it.

HOW DOES THIS WORK?

Let's explore a scenario where you encounter someone who is struggling with addiction. It's a moment that reveals how our conditioning shapes our perceptions and influences our actions.

For example, I used to believe that people who were struggling with addiction were weak. I had a lot of negative beliefs about them, such as "They're just not trying hard enough" and "They're not really interested in getting help." These beliefs were shaped by my conditioning, which included a few bad experiences in the past with people who were struggling with addiction.

However, I realized that my negative beliefs were holding me back. I wanted to be able to see people who were struggling with addiction as people who are worthy of compassion and help. So, I started to challenge my negative beliefs about people who struggle with addiction. I started by talking to them and learning about their experiences. I also started volunteering at a rehabilitation center, where I got to see firsthand the challenges that people who are struggling with addiction face.

It wasn't easy at first, but I kept challenging my negative beliefs and eventually I started to see people who were struggling with addiction in a new light. I realized that they are just like me, they—people who are trying to overcome a difficult challenge.

This experience taught me a valuable lesson about the power of our beliefs. If we believe that someone is weak or morally corrupt, then we're more likely to treat them that way. But if we believe that someone is worthy of compassion and help, then we're more likely to treat them that way.

THE CHART

The chart below shows the process of creating reality in a sequential way. It is important to remember that this is a simplified version that depicts the fundamentals of the process.

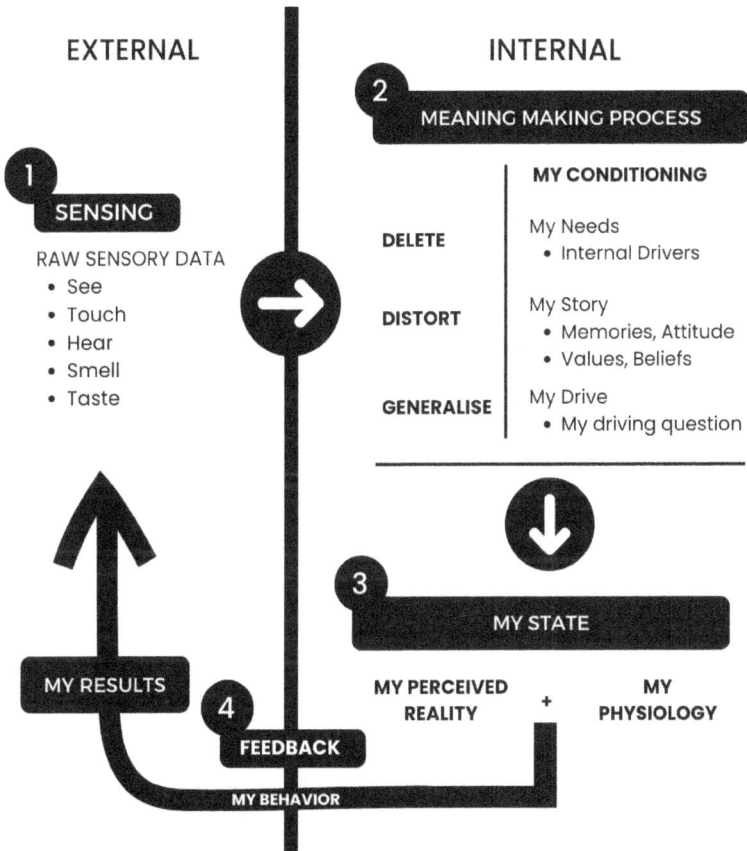

EXTERNAL   **INTERNAL**

2 MEANING MAKING PROCESS

MY CONDITIONING

1 SENSING

RAW SENSORY DATA
- See
- Touch
- Hear
- Smell
- Taste

DELETE — My Needs
- Internal Drivers

DISTORT — My Story
- Memories, Attitude
- Values, Beliefs

GENERALISE — My Drive
- My driving question

3 MY STATE

MY RESULTS

4 FEEDBACK

MY PERCEIVED REALITY + MY PHYSIOLOGY

MY BEHAVIOR

THE MIND'S MAGIC SHOW

Our reality is not what it seems. It is created inside-out, by our minds.

Step 1: Sensing

We perceive the world through our senses. We have five senses: sight, hearing, touch, taste, and smell. We also have a sixth sense, which is our intuition (but that's a whole other topic).

Our senses are like windows that allow us to see the world around us. But our minds are not just passive observers. They are also active editors. They process the information that we take in and make sense of it.

Step 2: Meaning-Making

Our minds are like editors. They analyze the information that we take in and make sense of it. Sometimes, our editors get a little overzealous and start deleting, distorting, and generalizing information.

- Deletion is the process of filtering out information that we don't want to see or hear. For example, if you're looking for your cellphone, you might delete the information that it's in your pocket. You might also delete the information that your spouse is listening to you right now.

- Distortion is the process of changing or twisting information to fit our beliefs or expectations. For example, if you're afraid of snakes, you might see a rope and think it's a snake. Or you might distort your spouse's words to make them sound more negative than they actually are.

- Generalization is the process of taking a single event and applying it to all events. For example, if your spouse doesn't listen to you once, you might think that they never listen to you. You might also generalize your negative experiences to make it seem like everyone in the world is against you.

Step 3: State Creation

After our minds have made sense of the information that we take in, they create a state. Our state is a blend of our mental, emotional, and physical conditions. It's like a cocktail, with our thoughts, beliefs, and expectations as the ingredients.

The ingredients in our state-cocktail can have a big impact on how we perceive the world. If we're feeling happy and confident, we're more likely to see the world through rose-colored glasses. But if we're feeling stressed or anxious, we're more likely to see the world through a dark cloud.

Step 4: The Feedback Loop

Our personal reality is a work in progress. It's constantly evolving, driven by our experiences, perspectives, and external feedback.

This feedback loop starts with our state of being. It's like a filter that we use to interpret the world around us.

Our state of being affects our behavior. When we're feeling positive and confident, we're more likely to take action and achieve our goals. But when we're feeling negative and anxious, we're more likely to procrastinate and give up.

Our behavior, in turn, shapes our results. The results that we achieve feed back into our state of being, creating a feedback loop.

So, if we want to change our personal reality, we need to change our feedback loop. We need to change our state of being and our behavior.

This can be challenging, but it's possible. By understanding the meaning-making process, we can gain awareness of how our minds shape our reality. Armed with this knowledge, we can intentionally craft a more positive and empowering personal reality.

Here are some examples of how our minds can distort information

- I saw a snake! (It was actually a rope.)

- My spouse never listens to me. (They actually listen to me most of the time.)

- Everyone in the world is against me. (That's not true. There are many people who care about me.)

SHIFTING OUR PERCEIVED REALITY: EMPOWERING CHANGE

Our reality is shaped by our filters. These filters are the beliefs, assumptions, and expectations that we hold about the world. They determine what we see, hear, and feel.

If our filters are negative, we'll see the world in a negative light. We'll be more likely to focus on the bad things and interpret events in a negative way. This can lead to a lot of stress, anxiety, and unhappiness.

But if we can change our filters, we can change our reality. We can start to see the world in a more positive light. We can focus on the good things and interpret events in a more positive way. This can lead to a lot of happiness, fulfillment, and success.

Here are some tips for shifting our perceived reality

1. Become aware of your filters. The first step is to become aware of the negative filters that you hold. Pay attention to your thoughts and feelings. When you notice a negative thought, ask yourself, "What filter am I using to see this situation?"

2. Challenge your filters. Once you're aware of your filters, you can start to challenge them. Ask yourself, "Is there any evidence to support this belief?" If not, you can start to reshape your belief.

3. Change your beliefs and expectations. The most powerful way to change our reality is to change our beliefs and expectations. When we change our beliefs, we change the way we interpret information. This, in turn, changes our emotions and behaviors.

For example, if you believe that you're not good enough, you'll interpret information in a way that confirms this belief. You'll focus on your mistakes and failures. But if you can change your belief to "I am capable and worthy," you'll start to interpret information in a more positive way. You'll focus on your successes and your potential.

SOCIAL MEDIA'S IMPACT ON OUR PERCEIVED REALITY

We've talked about how our filters shape our reality. Now, let's talk about something that most people struggle with: social media. Specifically, how it impacts our perceived reality.

SOCIAL MEDIA'S COMPARISON CIRCUS

Social media is a breeding ground for comparison culture. We're bombarded with carefully curated highlight reels of other people's lives, making us feel like we're falling short in comparison. It's a never-ending cycle of, "they have it, I don't." Talk about a downer, right?

Social media has taken the comparison game to a whole new level. It's like a mean kid from our childhood who just won't leave us alone. It invades our privacy, attacks our self-esteem, and makes us feel like we're in a constant battle to measure up. And let's not forget about those unrealistic, photoshopped images that mess with our heads. It's no wonder so many folks are struggling with their mental health these days.

Here's a little wisdom for you: A flower doesn't waste its time worrying about the flower next to it. It just blooms.

People often ask me, "Hey, how do you deal with all this comparison madness?"

To answer that, let me take you back to when I first started coaching. I felt the pressure to compare myself to all those big-shot practitioners out there. I was like a fish in a glass tank, constantly under the scrutiny of the public.

One day, during a mentoring session where this topic was front and center, my mentor, Sanjay Raghunath, dropped some serious truth bombs on me. He said, "Dhiren, you can't truly be something unless you've fully embraced it within yourself." And that, my friend, changed the way I saw things.

SHATTERING THE COMPARISON CYCLE WITH THE "DELETE, DISTORT, GENERALIZE" MODEL

I used to be a chronic comparer. I would compare myself to other people in every way imaginable. My looks, my intelligence, my success, my relationships: You name it, I compared it.

But one day, I had a breakthrough. I realized that comparing myself to others was actually making me unhappy. It was making me feel insecure and inadequate. And it was preventing me from living my own life to the fullest.

I started investigating my compulsion to compare through a different lens. I realized that it was all about deletion, distortion, and generalization.

Deletion is when we focus on the negative aspects of ourselves and ignore the positive ones. For example, I might focus on the fact that I'm not as strong as my friend, but I would ignore the fact that I'm faster and have read more than he has.

Distortion is when we exaggerate the negative aspects of ourselves and minimize the positive ones. For example, I might think that I haven't achieved much, even though I've achieved a lot in my life.

Generalization is when we take one negative experience and apply it to everything in our lives. For example, if I get rejected by one person, I might think that I'm unlovable.

Once I understood the "delete, distort, generalize" model, I was able to start breaking the comparison cycle. I started to focus on the positive aspects of myself. I stopped exaggerating the negative aspects of myself. And I stopped generalizing from one negative experience to everything in my life.

It wasn't easy, but it was worth it. Breaking the comparison cycle has helped me to become more confident and happier. I'm no longer afraid to be myself, and I'm no longer comparing myself to others.

FLIPPING THE COMPARISON GAME: DISTORT, COMPARE, AND LAUGH AT MY PAST SELF

One of the things that helped me to break the comparison cycle was to flip the comparison game. Instead of comparing myself to other people, I started comparing myself to my past self.

I would sit in a cozy armchair with a cup of tea in hand and reminisce about the good ol' days. I would think about all the things that I've accomplished since then, and I would laugh at my past self's questionable fashion choices.

It was a hilarious and insightful way to break the comparison cycle. It helped me to realize how far I've come, and it helped me to appreciate myself for who I am today.

COMPARING TO YOUR PAST SELF: A JOURNEY OF PROGRESS

So, when we talk about comparison, let's do it in a healthier and more fun way. Forget about comparing yourself to others and their seemingly perfect lives on social media. That's a recipe for disappointment and a one-way ticket to FOMO-land. Instead, let's focus on comparing yourself to the ultimate worthy opponent: your past self!

Think about it: Who better to challenge and inspire you than the person you were yesterday? When you compare yourself to your past self, it's like having your own personal cheerleader saying, "Look how far you've come, you awesome human!"

THE HONEST MIRROR

We saw how our conditioning, our senses, and our behavior all play a role in shaping our reality. We also saw how we can change our reality by changing our state of being and our behavior.

"The world is a mirror, and what you see in it is what you project."

— UNKNOWN

This quote reminds us that our reality is not fixed. It is constantly being created by our thoughts, beliefs, and actions. If we want to change our reality, we need to change our inner world.

THE POWER OF OUR THOUGHTS

Our thoughts are like waves. They create the ripples that shape our reality. If we want to create the reality we want, it's essential that our thoughts are aligned with the outcome we want.

THE POWER OF OUR BELIEFS

Our beliefs are like lenses. They filter the world around us and create our reality. If we have limiting beliefs, we will see the world through a lens of negativity and doubt. This will make it difficult to achieve our goals.

THE POWER OF OUR ACTIONS

Our actions are the final piece of the puzzle. If we want to change our reality, we need to take action. We need to build momentum by taking steps toward what we want.

CONCLUSION

The process of creating reality is not easy. It takes time, effort, and commitment. But it is possible. If we are willing to put in the work, we can create a reality that is full of joy, abundance, and love.

I hope this chapter has inspired you to start creating your own reality. Remember, the power is within you.

INNER GAME INTERVENTION REFLECTING ON MY PERCEIVED REALITY

Our reality is not what it seems. It is created inside-out, by our minds. Our conditioning, beliefs, and behaviors all play a role in shaping our reality.

Here are some questions you can ask yourself to reflect on your own reality:

- What is my current reality?

- How do I filter the information that I receive?

- How do I interpret the information that I receive?

- How do I make sense of the information that I receive?

- How is my state of being affecting my behavior?

- How are my results affecting my state of being?

- What changes do I need to make to my state of being, behavior, and results in order to create the reality that I want?

- What are the biggest challenges you are facing right now?

- What are your goals for the future?

- What are the beliefs and behaviors that are holding you back from achieving your goals?

A self-assessment tool
that you can use to evaluate how you think

Deletion:

- How often do you ignore information that is inconvenient or does not fit with your current beliefs?

- Do you find yourself focusing on the negative aspects of a situation and ignoring the positive?

- Do you find yourself making decisions based on your gut feeling rather than on the facts?

Distortion:

- How often do you see things in a way that is biased toward your own interests?

- Do you find yourself exaggerating or minimizing the importance of information?

- Do you find yourself interpreting information in a way that confirms your existing beliefs?

Generalization:

- How often do you make assumptions about people or situations based on limited information?

- Do you find yourself applying your own experiences to other people's situations?

- Do you find yourself making sweeping generalizations about groups of people?

Action:

Once you have reflected on these questions, take some action to create the reality you want. Here are some specific steps you can take:

- Set some goals for yourself.

- Make a list of the changes you want to make and start taking steps to make them happen.

- Find a mentor or coach who can support you on your journey.

- Join a support group or community of people who are also trying to make positive changes in their lives.

The Power of Change:

Remember, you have the power to change your reality. You are not a victim of your circumstances. You are the creator of your own life. By changing your beliefs, your behaviors, and your state of being, you can create a reality that is more aligned with your desires.

The Journey:

Creating a new reality is not always easy. It takes time, effort, and commitment. But it is possible. And it is worth it. Keep moving forward. And never, ever, ever, ever stop believing in yourself.

INTERVENTION

Inner Game Blueprint: If You Spot It, You Got It!

The concept of the "golden shadow" is a term coined by the Swiss psychiatrist Carl Jung, which refers to the positive traits and qualities that we see in others, but that we may not acknowledge or see in ourselves. When we "spot" a quality in another person and admire it, it can be an indication that we have that same quality within ourselves, but we are not aware of it or not expressing it fully.

The idea behind "if you spot it, you got it" is that what we see in others, whether positive or negative, is often a reflection of ourselves. If we are able to recognize and acknowledge our own positive qualities, we can work on developing and expressing them more fully, instead of feeling envious or comparing ourselves to others.

Here's a very powerful intervention to explore and integrate your golden shadow:

- Start by identifying a quality or trait in someone else that you admire or feel drawn to. It could be a friend, family member, colleague, or even a public figure.

- Ask yourself: "What is it about this person that I admire or feel drawn to?" Make a list of the qualities or traits that you see in them.

- Once you have your list, take a closer look at each quality and ask yourself: "Do I possess this quality within myself?" If so, acknowledge and celebrate it. If not, ask yourself: "Why not? What's holding me back from expressing this quality in my own life?"

- Choose one or two qualities that you identified that you would like to develop within yourself. Make a plan to practice expressing these qualities in your daily life.

- Finally, make a conscious effort to express appreciation and gratitude to the person who inspired you. This will help you integrate the qualities you admire in them and avoid projecting your own unacknowledged potential onto them.

By practicing these steps, you can learn to recognize and integrate the positive aspects of your personality that you may have overlooked or repressed in the past, thus embracing your "golden shadow."

CHAPTER 9

BOUNDARY SETTING

Saying No Without Feeling Guilty

BRING
IT
ON

"Boundaries are the invisible lines that define who we are and what we will and won't accept."

— ANNE KATHERINE

Are you a people pleaser? Are you stuck in the "Yes" trap? Do you have a knack for saying "yes" when every fiber of your being screams "NOOOO"? Are you trapped in a never-ending cycle of people-pleasing madness?

It's time to liberate!

Picture this: Someone asks you to do something you absolutely loathe. Maybe it's attending your fifth cousin's pet rock's birthday party.

Your instinct says "run," but your fear of disappointing or appearing rude takes over. Before you know it, you're muttering "yes" through gritted teeth, your soul weeping in agony.

But here's the kicker: saying "yes" to everything and everyone is a one-way ticket to the Land of Overwhelm. It's like juggling flaming chainsaws while riding a unicycle on a tightrope: stress, resentment, and a looming mental breakdown become your unwanted companions.

But fear not, my fellow "yes-aholics," you are not alone! A staggering eighty-five percent of people struggle with setting boundaries. It's like we all attended the same "How to Say No" training camp and got lost on the way to graduation.

In this chapter, we'll embark on a boundary-setting adventure together. We'll unleash the power of "no" without the guilt trip. You'll learn the art of saying "no" gracefully, setting boundaries like a boss, and reclaiming your sanity.

Get ready to slay the guilt and conquer the art of saying "no" with confidence. Your sanity will thank you.

Let's bring it on!

BOUNDARIES, THE SECRET TO SAYING "NO"

Boundaries are the limits we set for ourselves about how we want to be treated. They can be physical, emotional, or mental. When you set boundaries, you're saying, "This is what I'm willing to do, and this is what I'm not willing to do."

WHY ARE BOUNDARIES IMPORTANT?

Boundaries are important for our mental and emotional health. They help us to protect ourselves from harm and to live in accordance with our values. Emotional boundaries are a subset of boundaries that specifically deal with our emotions. They're the limits we set for ourselves about how we're willing to be treated emotionally.

NAVIGATING EMOTIONAL BOUNDARIES: A ROLLERCOASTER OF FEELINGS AND RESPONSES

Emotional boundaries aren't always clear-cut. Sometimes, we need to decipher the complex dance between our body's arousal and our mind's reaction to internal boundary violations. It's like trying to solve a Rubik's Cube while riding a unicycle on a tightrope: tricky, but oh-so-rewarding.

Imagine this: Someone tosses a sarcastic comment your way. Ouch! How does it make you feel? Belittled? Disrespected? Ridiculed? Or maybe it's a sting that tugs at your heartstrings. Whatever the case, your body releases cortisol, revving up your heart rate and blood pressure. It's a surefire sign of "dis-ease."

When I find myself in these situations, I have three options:

Option one: Cringe and tell myself I deserve it. Ah, the classic response of self-deprecation. But hey, let's hit the pause button here.

Option two: Cringe and ask myself if I deserve it. This is a more mindful approach. Take a moment to explore those thoughts and feelings.

Option three: Examine the source. Why would this person stoop to such sarcasm? What's their deal? Channel my inner detective and unearth the motivations behind the snark.

Option four: Remember to unpack it later. Sometimes, emotions need a little timeout before I can make sense of them. I take a breather, process, and then take action.

Option five: Try to understand why they feel the need to be sarcastic. It's a challenging response, but it's like donning an empathy cape, allowing us to tap into the other person's perspective.

Now, let's talk action!

Option one: I can smile and hide my feelings. A classic move to avoid conflict, but it doesn't quite tackle the underlying issue. Nice try, but not quite there.

Option two: I switch off, stonewall, and disengage from the conversation. Ah, the fortress of protection. It shields me from further hurt, but does it effectively communicate my boundaries? Not quite.

Option three: I can fire back with more sarcasm. It's a defense mechanism on steroids—but I should brace myself, because this response can escalate the conflict faster than a squirrel on a caffeine rush.

Option four: Walk away and leave the conversation. Now we're talking. This sends a crystal-clear message that I won't tolerate such behavior. *Mic drop*

Option five: I can understand the source of their inferiority, anger, or hurt, and stay engaged. Now, this is a challenge for the

BRING IT ON

brave-hearted. It's like wielding a double-edged sword, attempting to resolve the conflict while keeping my emotional fortress intact. Pro tip: Proceed with caution.

Remember, the best course of action depends on the situation and the individual. But here's the golden rule: We all have the right to set boundaries and protect our emotional well-being.

SETTING BOUNDARIES IN BUSINESS: WHERE EXPECTATIONS AND SANITY COLLIDE

Boundaries in business relationships are as crucial as boundaries in personal relationships. It's like having a sturdy fortress that keeps the chaos at bay and ensures smooth sailing in the treacherous waters of the corporate world. So, let's dive into the art of boundary-setting with a dash of humor and a sprinkle of wisdom!

Tip one: Be crystal clear about your expectations. Punctuality, meeting deadlines, and work quality are all part of the grand expectation extravaganza. Make sure your employees, clients, and colleagues are on the same page. After all, we don't want anyone wandering off into the land of "Oops, I had no idea!"

Tip two: Embrace your inner assertive superhero. When someone falls short of expectations, it's time to don that assertive cape. Communicate your needs with clarity and a hint of kindness (we don't want to traumatize anyone).

Tip three: Prepare to walk that talk. If all else fails and someone is stubbornly resistant to respecting your boundaries, it may be time to walk away. Walking away may seem drastic, but it's all about protecting your precious well-being. You deserve a drama-free zone.

NOW, LET'S UNLEASH A FEW MORE BOUNDARY-SETTING GEMS

Gem one: Set limits on your availability. Let them know you're not a 24/7 hotline. You need time to binge-watch your favorite shows and indulge in copious amounts of ice cream.

Gem two: Embrace the power of "no." It's a magical word that can save you from unnecessary stress and headaches. Don't feel guilty about declining requests that drain your time, energy, or expertise. No explanations are needed—just a firm, confident "no."

Gem three: Take those breaks, darling! Avoid burnout like the plague. Get up, stretch, breathe in some fresh air, or do a little happy dance. Your sanity will thank you.

Gem four: Delegate like a boss. When overwhelm hits, don't be afraid to hand off tasks to your trusty employees or colleagues. It's like unleashing a team of productivity superheroes while you focus on conquering the truly important stuff.

Remember, by fortifying your business relationships with clear expectations and the courage to enforce them, you'll create a workplace utopia of productivity and harmony.

FROM PEOPLE-PLEASER TO BOUNDARY NINJA: MY JOURNEY TO SELF-RESPECT

I used to be a people-pleaser. I feared hurting people so badly that I would do anything to avoid conflict. This meant I said yes when I meant no, became disconnected from my intuition, and led my team through an energy-draining year.

I ended up hurting them (and myself) far more than if I had been honest with myself earlier and changed things when they needed to be changed. It wasn't until I really looked at my people-pleaser shadow and came to terms with the part of me that desired to do things that made me happy—even if it initially required difficult conversations—that I was able to liberate myself from my old patterns.

The ultimate integration of my people-pleaser shadow was to integrate selfishness into my life and begin setting clear boundaries, choosing things I wanted, and living into my personal values. I integrated my people-pleaser with my selfishness and created a version of me who could choose myself without actively hurting others. I found a way to have loving, considerate, honest conversations that had everyone's best interest at heart.

KEY TAKEAWAYS FROM MY JOURNEY: EMBRACING SELFISHNESS, SETTING BOUNDARIES, AND HONESTY

Are you ready for some condensed wisdom that I've collected over the years?

Takeaway one: Embrace your inner selfishness (in a good way). Selfishness isn't the enemy of selflessness—it's about knowing what you want and going after it like a determined squirrel chasing acorns. So, be a little selfish.

Takeaway two: Give "no" a standing ovation. You don't have to be a "yes" machine, pumping out favors like a candy dispenser. It's okay to decline requests if you're running on empty or simply don't feel like it. Say "no" with gusto and reclaim your time and sanity.

Takeaway three: Honesty is the OG policy. Yes, it can be awkward and uncomfortable at times, like wearing shoes that are two sizes too small. But let those honest conversations flow, and watch your relationships flourish like a garden of laughter and understanding.

THE BIGGEST MISTAKE THAT CHANGED MY LIFE

My tendency to people-please, sacrificing my own needs and desires, led me to make a big mistake that changed my life forever. That was the decision to travel to London for a business deal when my wife, Jasmine, was expecting our first child.

Remember, even the biggest regrets can lead to important lessons. Missing the birth of my son was one of the biggest regrets of my life. I now know that it is important to put my own needs and desires first, even if it means saying no to people. I have also learned that it is okay to make mistakes, as long as I learn from them. This experience has made me a stronger person, and I am grateful for the lesson that it taught me.

THE BOUNDARY SETTING BREAKTHROUGH: SWAP "NO" FOR POLITE POWER

"No" is a mighty word, but let's give it a rest. If boundary-setting has you scratching your head, try these alternative phrases that are as gentle as a kitten's purr:

- I'll pass on that one, thank you.
- Maybe next time.
- I'll leave that one for now, thanks.
- I'm okay, seriously.

These words still pack a punch, but with a touch of politeness to spare. No offense, just good vibes.

KEY TAKEAWAY: NO BOUNDARIES + SILENT NO = NO TRANSFORMATION!

If you're eager to rock the world of boundaries and transform your life, here's the scoop: You've got to be assertive and crystal clear about your needs. Saying "no" is like the secret sauce of boundary-setting, but it's not the only ingredient in this recipe. You also need a healthy dose of standing up for yourself and enforcing those boundaries like a boss. It's time to turn those "No's" into the ultimate "Yes" to your own well-being.

THE YES-NO MODEL: BOUNDARIES WITH A DASH OF INTENTION

This model has been the ultimate boundary-setting hack.

The Yes-No model—a simple yet powerful approach to living a life that's intentional and boundary-driven. It's simple, yet profound:

Step one: Know thy priorities! What truly matters to you? Identify your top priorities like a boss.

Step two: Ask yourself, "Does this opportunity align with my priorities?" If the answer is a resounding "yes," proceed with a grin. If it's a hesitant "no," proceed with caution.

'Step three': The ultimate question—"Am I willing to say no to other things for this opportunity?" If your inner voice screams "no," it's time to channel your boundary-setting superhero and decline that invitation.

☀ CONCLUSION

"Boundaries are not about controlling others. They are about controlling ourselves and how we respond to others."

— CLOUD & TOWNSEND

Setting boundaries is an essential skill for anyone who wants to live a healthy and fulfilling life. It takes courage to set boundaries, but it is worth it. When we set boundaries, we are taking care of ourselves and our own needs. We are also setting ourselves up for success.

Now that you've learned the basics of setting boundaries, it's time to put your skills to the test. The following exercise will help you practice setting boundaries in a specific area of your life.

Take some time to complete the exercise, and then reflect on your experience. What did you learn about yourself? What challenges did you face? And what did you do to overcome those challenges?

By completing this exercise, you'll be one step closer to setting powerful boundaries and taking control of your well-being.

ⓘ INTERVENTION

Inner Game Blueprint: Unbreakable Boundaries

Mastering the Inner Game: A 10-Step Exercise to Set Powerful Boundaries and Take Control of Your Inner Game.

1. Start by identifying the areas in your life where you need to set boundaries. This could be in your personal relationships, work life, or any other area where you feel like your boundaries are being crossed.

2. Make a list of your personal values and priorities. This will help you identify what's important to you and what you want to protect.

3. Think about what specific boundaries you need to set in order to protect your values and priorities. For example, if you value your alone time, you may need to set boundaries around how much time you spend with friends and family.

4. Practice saying "no" in a kind but firm way. This will help you set boundaries and communicate your needs clearly. For example, if a friend asks you to do something that you don't have the time or energy for, say something like "I appreciate the invitation, but I'm not able to do that right now."

5. Be consistent and follow through on your boundaries. This will help you establish a pattern of behavior that communicates your needs clearly and helps others respect your boundaries.

6. Identify any fears or limiting beliefs that might be holding you back from setting boundaries. Common fears may include the fear of rejection or the fear of conflict. Once you've identified these fears, challenge them by questioning whether they are really true or whether they are just assumptions you've made.

7. Practice self-care regularly. This could be anything that helps you feel more centered and grounded, such as meditation, exercise, or spending time in nature. When you take care of yourself, you're better able to identify your needs and set boundaries that support your well-being.

8. Be open and honest with the people in your life about your boundaries. Let them know what you need and why it's important to you. When you communicate clearly and honestly, others are more likely to respect your boundaries.

9. Practice mindfulness when setting boundaries. Take a moment to check in with yourself and ask whether a particular request or situation feels aligned with your values and priorities. If it doesn't, consider setting a boundary to protect your needs.

10. Finally, be patient with yourself. Setting boundaries is a process, and it can take time to get comfortable with it. Remember that every small step you take is progress, and you are worth the effort it takes to protect your well-being.

CHAPTER 10

CRUSHING SHAME
WITH VULNERABILITY

BRING
IT
ON

Ever done something so cringeworthy that you wanted to crawl into a black hole of eternal embarrassment? Yeah, we've all been there.

As a kid, I was the designated target of bullies, leaving me feeling like a shriveled-up raisin of shame. I cowered in fear of judgment, fearing that every eye was dissecting my every move.

It took me a few years, but I can say I'm shame-free now.

It all started with a bold move—an Instagram post that spilled the beans on my bully-ridden past. I bared my soul, revealing the dark corners of shame and inadequacy that haunted me. I was floored by the response. People poured in with their own tales of shame and healing, creating a chorus of vulnerability. Turns out, we're all in this together.

In this chapter, we will navigate the treacherous waters of shame with humor, grit, and a hefty dose of self-acceptance.

Let's bring it on!

SHAME AND JUDGMENT: UNLEASHING THE FEARLESSNESS WITHIN

Shame and fear of judgment—they're like the dynamic duo of emotional havoc. They can hold us hostage, making us feel like a bunch of misfit toys in a world of shiny superheroes.

Picture this: I was a bully magnet as a kid. I was trapped in a fear-fueled cage, terrified of failure, rejection, and becoming the star of a cringe-worthy comedy show. It felt like I had an invisible audience, critiquing my every move.

But then, a light bulb moment in adulthood illuminated the path to freedom. I rewound to my childhood, revisiting those moments of deep shame. I saw the false beliefs I had adopted—that I was a failure, unworthy of love.

I called BS on those beliefs. I told myself the truth: I am no failure. I am worthy of love, acceptance, and all the goodness life has to offer. I reached out to my ten-year-old self, whispering words of love and support. It wasn't easy, but with each step, my confidence grew. I held my head high, my ego humbled, and the fear of putting myself out there began to fade.

SHAME AND THE INNER GAME

Shame is a basic human emotion that we all experience at some point in our lives. It can be triggered by a variety of things, such as being bullied, rejected, or failing at something.

When we experience shame, it can feel like we're worthless, inadequate, or not good enough. This can lead to feelings of isolation, anxiety, and depression.

But shame doesn't have to control our lives. We can learn to overcome it by understanding how it works and by developing healthy coping mechanisms.

One way to overcome shame is to challenge the negative beliefs that we associate with it. For example, if we believe that we don't belong because we were bullied as a child, we can challenge that belief by reminding ourselves of the support and love we receive from family and friends.

THE POWER OF VULNERABILITY

Albert Einstein was told by his schoolteacher that he would never amount to anything. This was a devastating blow to the young Einstein, who was already struggling with his schoolwork. But Einstein refused to let the words of his teacher define him. He was determined to prove his teacher wrong, and he went on to become one of the most brilliant scientists of all time.

What was the difference between Einstein and the other students who were told they would never amount to anything? The difference was that Einstein was willing to be vulnerable. He was willing to expose his failures and his doubts. And it was this vulnerability that allowed him to grow and learn.

When we are vulnerable, we are open to new experiences. We are open to learning and growing. And we are open to connection with others. Vulnerability is not weakness. It is strength. It is the courage to be ourselves, even when we are afraid.

So, if you want to live a full and fulfilling life, don't be afraid to be vulnerable. Embrace your failures and doubts. They are the footholds to growth and learning. And they are the key to connecting with others on a deeper level.

UNLEASH THE POWER OF VULNERABILITY: LET'S GET REAL!

Ready to dive headfirst into the world of vulnerability? Here's the bite-sized guide to unleashing your vulnerable superhero:

Step one: Embrace the honesty within. Face those fears and doubts with a raised eyebrow and a knowing nod. Be honest with yourself, and watch the magic unfold.

Step two: Share the juicy bits. Open up to others and spill the beans about your fears and doubts. Brace yourself for surprising acceptance and unwavering support. It's like finding a tribe of understanding unicorns!

As you bask in the glorious light of vulnerability, behold the perks that await. Acceptance, love, connection, and fulfillment—they're all within reach. Say hello to a life well-lived.

Now, let's tackle those pesky shame intruders:

One: Give your feelings a nod. Admit that shame has crashed the party. Don't try to sweep it under the rug—acknowledge its presence like a cool cat.

Two: Crush those negative thoughts. Challenge the lies you tell yourself and replace them with compassionate reality checks. It's like being your own myth-busting superhero.

Three: Shower yourself with self-compassion. Be your own BFF and remember that mistakes are part of the human experience. Forgive yourself, move forward, and embrace your imperfectly perfect self.

Four: Connect like a social butterfly. Shame loves to isolate, but you're too savvy for that. Seek out those who embrace you for who you are—your fellow warriors in the battle against shame.

Five: Seek professional backup if needed. Sometimes the shame war requires reinforcements. Coaches, mentors and resources are there to guide you through, offering tools and insights for a shame-free life.

THE VULNERABILITY EXPEDITION

I encourage you to be more vulnerable in your own life. Start by sharing your failures and doubts with someone you trust. Evaluate how it feels to be open and honest with them. You may be surprised at how much you learn about yourself from the experience.

I also challenge you to be more vulnerable in your work. Share and execute your ideas. They don't have to be perfect: they never are. Seek feedback; it's in the openness to feedback that we learn and grow.

One of those platforms where I am able to embrace vulnerability is in the Entrepreneurs Organization, a global organization of like-minded entrepreneurs, where business-minded adventurers come together to conquer personal challenges and unlock new opportunities!

Within the organization lies a safe space known as The Forum— where members share their triumphs, tribulations, and yes, even their elusive five percent.

WHAT IS FIVE PERCENT?

Picture this: You're cruising through life, tackling your entrepreneurial endeavors with all the finesse of a trapeze artist. But amidst the glamour and glory, there's a small corner of your mind, a hidden treasure trove of thoughts and feelings that you've guarded like a fiercely protected secret.

We call it the five percent, because it's that sliver of vulnerability we often keep under lock and key.

Within the forum, I've embraced the power of sharing my five percent. It's a space where superheroes strip off their capes and reveal their human side.

Here, I have spilled my guts (figuratively, of course) and laid bare my doubts, fears, insecurities and failures.

It's like witnessing a magician divulge their most coveted tricks—a moment of raw honesty and vulnerability that leaves us awestruck.

Imagine the scene: Entrepreneurs from all walks of life, sitting in a circle, sharing their innermost thoughts and feelings.

One by one, I peeled back the layers, revealing my personal struggles, moments of self-doubt, and the demons I'm battling with.

And as each member bares their soul, something magical happens. The room crackles with energy, bonds strengthen, and the weight of vulnerability is lifted. These moments are like precious gems, shimmering with the power of connection and growth.

We realize that we're not alone in our struggles. We find solace in the shared experiences of fellow adventurers who have weathered similar storms.

It's like stumbling upon a hidden oasis in the vast desert of entrepreneurship—a place where we can quench our thirst for understanding and support.

I invite you to embrace the magic of safe spaces like a forum where you can reveal your five percent.

Dare to expose those thoughts and feelings you've kept hidden away.

You'll be amazed at the resilience and strength that lie beneath the surface.

Embrace the vulnerability, where five percent becomes the catalyst for extraordinary growth!

AN ENTREPRENEUR'S HIT OF SHAME

Enter the Shame HIT, the heavyweight champion of shame-induced feelings. It's that gut-wrenching sensation we experience when we fall short of our own sky-high expectations or those set by others.

Think humiliation, embarrassment, and a sprinkle of worthlessness thrown in for good measure.

The Shame HIT can be triggered by a multitude of mishaps: making a blunder, receiving criticism, or facing rejection head-on.

When it strikes, our bodies go into overdrive, releasing a tsunami of stress hormones that wreak havoc on our physical and emotional well-being.

THE SHAME OF FAILURE

Once upon a time, in the unpredictable realm of entrepreneurship, I embarked on a business venture that held the promise of greatness.

With dreams of success and a team of dedicated employees by my side, I forged ahead, braving the twists and turns of the market.

But alas, fate had a different plan in store. Despite their valiant efforts, unforeseen challenges arose, and the business began to lose its footing.

The once-thriving enterprise started to waver under the weight of the pandemic and a shift in government regulation, leaving me with a difficult decision to make.

With a heavy heart, I realized that the business was no longer viable, and the time had come to shut its doors. This meant bidding farewell to the dedicated individuals who had poured their time, energy, and passion into the company's growth.

The weight of responsibility rested on my shoulders as I had to deliver the news and let go of people who had been on the journey with me from day one. As the reality sank in, so too did the waves of shame. Doubts flooded my mind, whispering tales of inadequacy and failure.

The shame of not being able to sustain the business, of disappointing the loyal team they had assembled, threatened to overshadow the achievements and hard work that had come before.

OVERCOMING SHAME

But amidst the darkness of shame, a glimmer of strength emerged. I realized that failure is not a reflection of my worth or ability, but an inherent part of the unpredictable journey of entrepreneurship.

The decision to let go of the business and its employees was not an admission of defeat, but a courageous act of resilience and responsibility.

With this newfound perspective, I mustered the courage to face my team. They gathered together, bearing the weight of the news, and delivered it with honesty, transparency, and genuine gratitude.

The room was filled with mixed emotions—sadness, uncertainty, and perhaps a touch of relief. Yet, amidst the bittersweet farewell, a sense of camaraderie and support prevailed.

As the days turned into weeks, and weeks into months, I navigated the aftermath of the business closure with resilience and grace. I took the time to reflect on the lessons learned, the growth experienced, and the invaluable relationships forged. Through introspection and self-compassion, the suffocating grip of shame began to loosen, replaced by a sense of pride in the journey taken.

For in the tapestry of entrepreneurship, success and failure are interwoven threads. It is the courage to embrace both and the ability to rise from the ashes that define a true entrepreneur.

The shame dissipated, and I held my head high. My journey was far from over; it had merely taken an unexpected turn.

As we navigate the uncharted path ahead, remember that failure does not define us—our resilience and determination do.

Have you ever been afraid to be yourself?

I know I have. I used to be terrified of being vulnerable. I was afraid of being judged, of being rejected, of being seen as weak.

My fear of vulnerability was so strong that it kept me from living my life to the fullest.

I remember one time, I was invited to speak at a conference. I was so excited about the opportunity, but I was also terrified. I knew that I would be putting myself out there, and I was afraid of what people would think of me. I spent weeks rehearsing my speech, and I even hired a coach to help me overcome my fear of public speaking.

On the day of the conference, I was so nervous that I could barely eat. I felt like I was going to be sick. But I took a deep breath and went on stage. And you know what? It went great! I spoke from the heart, and I connected with the audience. I realized that I was capable of being vulnerable and that it didn't mean that I was weak.

Overcoming my fear of vulnerability was one of the best things I've ever done. It's allowed me to live my life more fully and authentically. And it's helped me to connect with others on a much deeper level.

VULNERABILITY: THE JOURNEY CONTINUES

- Vulnerability can be scary, but it is also necessary for growth, learning and connection. These are also its benefits.

- There are many ways to be vulnerable, such as sharing our thoughts and feelings, taking risks, and being open to feedback.

- Vulnerability is a journey, not a destination. It takes time and practice to be more vulnerable.

CONCLUSION

"Vulnerability is the birthplace of innovation, creativity, and change."

— BRENÉ BROWN

Shame is a powerful emotion that can hold us back from living our lives to the fullest. But it doesn't have to control us. By understanding how shame works and by developing healthy coping mechanisms, we can overcome it and embrace vulnerability.

Vulnerability is not weakness. It is strength. It is the courage to be ourselves, even when we are afraid. When we are vulnerable, we are open to new experiences, learning, and growth. We are also open to connecting with others on a deeper level.

INNER GAME INTERVENTION: THE SHAME SPIRAL INTERVENTION

This intervention is designed to help you identify the negative thoughts and beliefs that are associated with your shame. It will also help you challenge those thoughts and beliefs, and to start to replace them with more positive ones.

Step 1: Reflect on a time when you felt ashamed.

- What were the specific events that led up to your feeling of shame?

- What were the negative thoughts and beliefs that you were having at the time?

Step 2: Challenge the negative thoughts and beliefs.

- Ask yourself if there is any evidence to support those thoughts and beliefs.

- Are they really true?

- Are there other ways to interpret the situation?

Step 3: Replace the negative thoughts and beliefs with more positive ones.

- What are your strengths and accomplishments?

- What are the things that you are good at?

- Remind yourself of these things when you start to feel ashamed.

Step 4: Focus on building your self-esteem.

- Who are the supportive people that you surround yourself with, who lift you?

- How often are you focused on your positive qualities and on the things that you are grateful for?

This exercise can be helpful to overcome shame.

With practice, you will be able to challenge the negative thoughts and beliefs that are associated with your shame, and to start to replace them with more positive ones.

CHAPTER 11

HOW TO STAY RELEVANT IN THE AGE OF AI

BRING
IT
ON

Feeling like a stressed-out squirrel in a world of rapid change and mind-boggling advancements? Take a deep breath, because amidst the chaos, there's a silver lining: adaptability.

The world is spinning faster than ever. New technologies are popping up like mushrooms after a rainstorm. Our work and lifestyle are being catapulted into uncharted territories. It's like trying to navigate a whirlwind.

If we resist the winds of change, we risk being left behind in a cloud of outdated irrelevance. Adaptation is the secret ingredient to survival in this age of AI and constant transformation.

Let's get real for a moment. Adaptation isn't always a walk in the park. It's like trying to learn a new dance routine on roller skates. It can be overwhelming, downright intimidating even. However, with a few strategic moves, we can conquer the challenges that lie ahead.

In this chapter, we will discuss how we can adapt and go from relevance to flourishing.

Let's bring it on!

THE HUMAN EDGE IN THE AGE OF AI

In the age of AI, we are faced with a new challenge: How to stay relevant in a world where machines are becoming increasingly capable. We can no longer rely on our ability to do things that machines can do better. Instead, we need to focus on our unique human qualities.

What makes us human? What are the qualities that machines cannot replicate?

HERE ARE A FEW IDEAS

- Adaptability: We are able to change and adjust to new situations.

- Creativity: We are able to come up with new ideas and solutions.

- Empathy: We are able to understand and connect with others.

- Problem-solving: We are able to think critically and solve problems.

- Communication: We are able to communicate effectively with others.

- Social intelligence: We are able to understand and navigate social interactions.

Throughout this book, we have discussed some of the qualities that make us human. In the age of AI, we need to embrace our humanity and focus on these qualities. We need to be creative, empathetic, problem-solvers, communicators, and socially intelligent. If we do this, we will be able to thrive in a world where machines are becoming increasingly capable. In this chapter, we will dive into what I believe is the most critical human quality in the age of AI—adaptability.

MASTERING THE ART OF ADAPTABILITY: UNLEASHING YOUR INNER GAME IN THE AGE OF AI

In this era of AI wonders, adaptability has become the chameleon of life skills—shifting colors and seamlessly adjusting to new situations like a boss. It's more crucial than ever to level up your adaptability game and embrace the winds of change with open arms.

It all starts with a mindset shift—a radical acceptance that change is the new normal. Instead of resisting, picture yourself as a seasoned surfer, fearlessly riding the waves of transformation with style and a mischievous grin.

Adaptation isn't just about survival; it's about thriving and finding your unique place in this AI-infused world.

In this game of adaptation, flexibility is your ultimate secret weapon. Think outside the box—or better yet, imagine there is no box at all! The Age of AI calls for a willingness to adapt, learn, explore, and find your groove amidst the chaos.

HERE ARE SOME ADDITIONAL LESSONS THAT HAVE DEVELOPED MY ADAPTABILITY

- **Open the Door to New Adventures:** I've tried to always shake things up, by embracing new experiences, meeting peculiar people, and learning funky skills. I expose myself to the weird and wonderful.

- **Hug my Mistakes:** Face it—we all mess up from time to time. The secret sauce for me has been to squeeze every drop of wisdom out of those slip-ups.

- **Become a Master of Adaptation:** Plans don't always unfold as we would like them to, it's essential to be flexible when they don't.

Adaptability isn't about being the perfect, robotic version of yourself. It's about being as beautifully flawed and authentic as a Picasso masterpiece. It's about embracing change with open arms, seeing it as a playground for personal growth, and staying true to your values as the world around you does the cha-cha-cha.

THE IMPORTANCE OF ADAPTABILITY IN ENDURANCE SPORTS

I am an endurance athlete who loves to push my limits. However, my performance started to suffer when I noticed strange changes in my body. I was tired, bloated, and my energy levels were low. After some investigation, I learned that I was intolerant to dairy. This was a challenge, but I decided to adapt my diet and adopt a vegan lifestyle.

At first, it was difficult to give up dairy products. I loved cheese, creamy desserts, and milk in my coffee. But I knew that if I wanted to improve my health and performance, I had to make a change.

I started by researching plant-based alternatives to dairy products. I found that there are many delicious and nutritious options available. I also found a supportive community of vegan athletes who helped me along the way.

After a few months, I started to see the benefits of my dietary change. My sleep improved, my bloating disappeared, and my energy levels soared. I was able to train harder and longer than ever before.

This experience taught me the importance of adaptability. When we are able to embrace change and adapt to new situations, we are better able to thrive in the face of what seem insurmountable challenges.

THE IMPORTANCE OF ADAPTABILITY IN MORNING ROUTINES

I am a morning person who believes that the first few hours of the day set the tone for the rest of it. I used to have a rigid morning routine, but I learned that adaptability is essential for success.

I started by allowing for flexibility in my schedule and being more compassionate with myself if I didn't stick to my routine perfectly. I also learned to be more mindful of my needs and circumstances, and I made adjustments to my routine accordingly.

Over time, my morning routine has evolved into a personalized practice that catered to my unique needs and ever-changing circumstances. I realized that adaptability and resilience were the cornerstones of a successful routine. This allowed me to embrace the unpredictability of life and make necessary adjustments.

THE IMPORTANCE OF ADAPTABILITY: A HILARIOUSLY FLEXIBLE MORNING ROUTINE

Now, let me take you through my morning routine. It's a routine I like to call my "Morning ROOTine" (see what I did there?) because it's all about grounding myself and preparing for whatever the day throws at me. So, here's the breakdown:

- **Rise at 4:00 a.m.:** Yes, you heard that right. I willingly subject myself to the unholy hour of 4.00 a.m.

- **Focus on my "WHY" statement:** I have this plaque on my nightstand with my "WHY" statement, a profound reminder of my purpose and goals.

- **Talk to myself in the mirror:** Oh, you thought I was done with the weirdness? Think again! I stand in front of the mirror and have a pep talk with myself, telling myself how much I love me.

- **Breathwork extravaganza:** I do two types of breathwork. First up, we have "Box breathing." It's a fancy four-cycle breathing exercise that helps me relax and focus. It's like my own little Zen moment before the chaos ensues. Then, for added excitement, we move on to "Kundalini breathing." It's a more vigorous exercise that energizes me and clears my mind.

- **Meditation, because why not?** This is by far the single most important habit I have developed; it's the difference that's made all the difference.

- **Get physical for 60 minutes:** After all that inner peace, it's time to break a sweat. I engage in some form of physical activity for a whole hour where I either run, bike, swim, or engage in strength training.

- **Journal like nobody's reading:** I wrap up my routine with a blissful 10 minutes of journaling. It's my chance to reflect on the previous day's triumphs and tribulations while setting my intentions for the day ahead.

- **I send a daily email to my kids,** a habit that I developed a few months after they were born.

Now, here's the key to this wild morning routine—I'm adaptable. I'm not rigid about the sequence or timing. Life throws curveballs, and I'm ready to dodge them. If I need to adjust or shuffle things around, I'm up for it. The goal is to complete all the activities, even if it means a little improvisation along the way.

If I were too rigid, I'd be as stressed as a cat in a bathtub. But with adaptability, I can roll with the punches and stay calm.

THE INNER GAME AND AI

The Inner Game is the mental and emotional state that we bring to our work and our lives. It is the foundation of our resilience, our creativity, and our ability to adapt to change.

In the age of AI, the Inner Game is even more important. AI is a powerful tool, but it is not a replacement for human ingenuity, creativity, and empathy. We need to be able to use AI to our advantage, and we need to be able to protect ourselves from its potential dangers.

The Inner Game can help us to do both of these things. By developing our inner resilience, we can become more resistant to the negative effects of AI. By developing our inner creativity, we can find new ways to use AI to benefit humanity. And by developing our inner empathy, we can ensure that AI is used in a way that is ethical and responsible.

HOW TO ADAPT TO THE AGE OF AI

So, how do we adapt to the age of AI? Here are a few tips:

- **Be willing to experiment:** Try new things and take risks. Failure is a part of learning, so don't be afraid to make mistakes.

- **Be flexible:** Be able to change your plans and strategies as needed. The world is constantly changing, so we need to be able to adapt to it.

- **Be open to feedback:** Feedback is a valuable tool for learning and improving. When we're open to feedback, we're more likely to identify areas where we need to improve and make changes.

- **Be patient:** Change takes time. Don't expect to be an expert overnight. Just keep learning and adapting, and you'll eventually reach your goals.

- **Develop your Inner Game:** The Inner Game is the foundation of our ability to adapt to change. By developing our inner resilience, creativity, and empathy, we can become more resistant to the negative effects of AI and find new ways to use AI to benefit humanity.

CONCLUSION

"The only way to predict the future is to create it."

— PETER DRUCKER

In today's world, change is the only constant. The ability to adapt is essential for success. In the age of AI, adaptability is more important than ever. We need to be able to embrace change, be open to new experiences, and be flexible in our thinking. We also need to be patient and persistent, as adaptability takes time and practice.

INTERVENTIONS

In this section, we will discuss two exercises/interventions that can help you practice adaptability. The first exercise is called "Inner Game Blueprint: Step outside your comfort zone." The second exercise is called "Questions to Consider."

Inner Game Blueprint: Step Outside Your Comfort Zone

This exercise helps you practice being open to new solutions and taking risks. It is a great way to challenge yourself and grow as a person.

To do this exercise, you will need to identify a situation where you feel stuck or resistant to change. It could be related to work, relationships, or personal goals. Once you have identified the situation, you will need to write down three possible solutions to the situation. However, the catch is that these solutions must be completely outside of your comfort zone.

For example, if you're struggling with a work project, one solution could be to ask a coworker from a different department for help, even if you don't know them very well.

Once you have written down three solutions, you will need to choose one of them and implement it. Remember, this should be something that challenges you and pushes you out of your comfort zone.

After trying out the solution, you will need to reflect on what you learned. Did it work? Did you learn something new about yourself or the situation? How did you feel about trying something new?

☺ QUESTIONS TO CONSIDER

This exercise helps you think about the challenges and opportunities that AI presents. It is a great way to start a conversation about the future of AI and how we can use it in a positive way.

To do this exercise, you will need to consider the following questions:

- What are some of the challenges of adapting to change in the age of AI?

- How can we develop a strong inner game that will help us adapt to change?

- What are some specific tips for how to use AI in a positive way?

- How can we ensure that AI is used in an ethical and responsible way?

- What are some of the potential impacts of AI on the future of humanity?

- What role do you think humans will play in the age of AI?

I hope you find these exercises/interventions helpful. By practicing adaptability, you can become more resilient and better able to thrive in the age of AI.

CHAPTER 12

THE HABIT THAT HAS MADE ALL THE DIFFERENCE

BRING
IT
ON

THE MONKEY MIND:
TAMING THE WILD THOUGHTS

Ever feel like your mind is running a marathon while you're trying to sit still? Like a monkey swinging from one thought branch to another, leaving you feeling frazzled and unable to focus? Well, join the club! The Monkey Mind is a common condition that plagues many of us, making relaxation and concentration feel like distant dreams.

I've been there. For the better part of my life, my mind resembled a Formula One race, zooming at full speed and leaving me feeling like a helpless spectator. Anxiety and sleepless nights became my unwelcome companions, and I struggled to find peace amidst the mental chaos.

I tried everything under the sun to rein in my racing thoughts, from meditation to therapy to consuming copious amounts of chamomile tea (I think I single-handedly boosted the global chamomile industry). But despite my efforts, my Monkey Mind just wouldn't quit swinging.

However, one fateful day, the stars aligned, and I discovered a game-changing practice. A simple yet powerful tool that helped me tame my unruly mind and brought me back to the present moment.

This tool has dissolved a tremendous amount of struggle and anxiety for me, and I have no doubt it will do the same for you.

THE POWER OF FOCUS

I used to be terrible at focusing. My mind would always wander, and I would find it difficult to stay on task, which led to me feeling stressed and anxious. I would often procrastinate on work or school assignments, and I would sometimes even forget what I was supposed to be doing.

But then I learned that focus is a skill that can be learned and developed. And I believe that focus is essential for our mental health. When we're able to focus, we're better able to manage our thoughts and emotions. We're also better able to cope with difficult situations.

There are many ways to improve our focus. Here are two of my favorites:

Meditation: Meditation is a great way to train our minds to focus. There are many different types of meditation, but the most important thing is to find one that works for you. I personally like to focus on my breath, but you could also focus on a mantra or a visualization.

Mental rehearsal: Visualizing yourself performing a task or activity in a successful way can help you improve your focus and performance. For example, if you're giving a presentation, you could visualize yourself delivering it smoothly and confidently. Or, if you're taking a test, you could visualize yourself answering all the questions correctly.

I've found that these two techniques have helped me to improve my focus immensely. I'm still not perfect, I keep reminding myself that this is an infinite game.

MEDITATION

Meditation is a broad term that encompasses a wide range of practices. There are many different ways to meditate, and the best way for you will depend on your individual needs and preferences. Some people find that sitting quietly and focusing on their breath is the most effective way to meditate, while others prefer to use guided meditations or mantras.

THE ZEN SEEDS

When it comes to focused and centered individuals, I can't help but look at my sister and my mom. They're like Zen masters in a world of chaos, effortlessly gliding through life with a sense of calm that I can only dream of. And you know what's even more impressive? They're the happiest and most content people I know. It's like they've discovered the secret to eternal bliss, and I'm over here still searching for my car keys.

But here's the common thread that ties them together: they've both been devout practitioners of meditation for as long as I can remember. It's like they have a direct hotline to the universe's customer service, and they've learned how to navigate life's ups and downs with grace and tranquility.

I couldn't help but be intrigued by their peaceful aura and unwavering composure. It's like they subtly conditioned me into the world of meditation, planting those Zen seeds in my mind.

MEDITATION: A LIFESAVER

I started meditating 15 years ago, and it has been a transformative journey. It has helped me to manage my thoughts and emotions, improve my focus and concentration, and to find stillness amidst the chaos.

My meditation practice has not been without its challenges. There have been times when my mind has been like a wild rodeo, bucking and kicking, trying to throw me off balance. But through it all, I have learned to embrace the quirks and imperfections of my practice. It's not about achieving the perfect lotus position or attaining instant enlightenment. It's about embracing the journey—the bumps, the hiccups, and the rogue sneezes.

Meditation has been a lifesaver for me. It has helped me to become more mindful, more present, and more grateful. I am grateful for the opportunity to share my journey with you, and I hope that you will find it helpful.

THE HABIT THAT HAS MADE
ALL THE DIFFERENCE

As Dan Harris says, "Meditation is like mental hygiene. We go to the gym to exercise our muscles; we meditate to exercise our brain." Meditation is a way of training our attention and awareness. It helps us to become more aware of our thoughts and emotions, and to let go of those that are not helpful.

One of the benefits of meditation is self-awareness. When we are more aware of our thoughts and emotions, we are better able to manage them. This can lead to a calmer, more peaceful mind.

In a 2009 interview with Oprah Winfrey, The Dalai Lama said, "To be aware of a single shortcoming in oneself is more useful than to be aware of a thousand in someone else." Meditation can help us to become more aware of our own shortcomings so that we can work on them. In addition to self-awareness, meditation also helps us to achieve mental fitness. Meditation trains our minds to be singularly focused, helping us to be more productive, creative, and resilient.

Sharon Salzberg's book, *Real Happiness: The Power of Meditation to Change Your Life* (2011) says, "Meditation is not a way of making your mind quiet. It's a way of entering into the quiet that's already there—buried under the 50,000 thoughts the average person thinks every day." Meditation helps us to get to the root of our thoughts and emotions so that we can experience true peace and well-being.

Meditation and mental rehearsal are two powerful tools that have helped me improve my self-awareness, mental fitness and performance.

MENTAL REHEARSAL

Have you ever visualized yourself performing a task or activity in a successful way? If so, you've already experienced the power of mental rehearsal. Mental rehearsal is a technique that can be used to improve performance in a variety of tasks. It involves visualizing yourself performing the task or activity in a successful way, step-by-step. This can help you to become more confident and to overcome challenges.

BENEFITS OF MENTAL REHEARSAL

There are many benefits to mental rehearsal. It can help you to:

- Improve your focus and concentration.
- Reduce anxiety and stress.
- Increase your motivation and self-confidence.
- Improve your performance in a variety of tasks.

MY PUBLIC SPEAKING ANXIETY: FROM BUTTERFLIES TO STANDING OVATIONS

When it comes to public speaking, well, let's just say it's been a wild rollercoaster ride of nerves, sweaty palms, and a heart that's racing like it's in a marathon.

Picture this: I had a big talk coming up, and when I say big, I mean standing-in-front-of-a-crowd-of-200-people big. Now, here's the kicker: I actually knew some of those people in the audience. Cue the internal pressure and the endless loop of thoughts telling me, "Don't mess this up, don't mess this up!"

As the fateful day approached, my anxiety decided to throw a party in my stomach. The butterflies were flapping their wings like they were training for the Olympics, and I couldn't seem to find an off switch. Sleeping? Forget about it. I was tossing and turning all night, running through worst-case scenarios in my mind.

Desperate for a solution, I turned to deep breathing exercises. You know, the ones they say can magically calm you down? Well, let me tell you, those breaths had the impact of a feather on an elephant. I was still a ball of nerves, and my stomach seemed to be channeling a not-so-friendly volcano.

But then, in my hour of desperation, I remembered a little technique called mental rehearsal. I decided to give it a go, because, at this point, I was willing to try anything that would keep my stomach from launching a protest.

So, I closed my eyes and visualized the talk. But not just any visualization, mind you. I went all out, creating a mental movie of me delivering the perfect talk. I saw myself up there, calm as a cucumber, oozing confidence. The audience? Well, they were hanging onto my every word, nodding with approval and even throwing in a few enthusiastic "amens."

I replayed this cinematic masterpiece in my mind several times, each time tweaking and refining the details. I started to feel a glimmer of confidence creeping in, like a tiny superhero ready to save the day.

Fast forward to the big moment. Sure, I still had a hint of nerves, but thanks to my mental rehearsal, I was able to keep my cool. I stepped up to that podium like a boss, and boy, did I deliver. The audience was captivated, engaged, and dare I say, they even threw in a few laughs at my well-timed jokes. Post-talk, I received compliments that made me walk out of there with a skip in my step.

Now, here's a nugget of wisdom for you: When it comes to mental rehearsal, go all in. Visualize every detail—what you'll say, how you'll move, even how you'll feel. Make it as realistic as a blockbuster movie, minus the explosions and car chases. And most importantly, repeat, repeat, repeat. It's like practicing your Oscar acceptance speech in front of the mirror, only this time, it's for real-life situations.

MEDITATION AND MENTAL REHEARSAL: A JOURNEY

I've been using both meditation and mental rehearsal for a few years now, and I've seen a huge difference in my life. I'm more aware of my thoughts and emotions, which has helped me to manage stress and anxiety more effectively. I'm also more focused and productive, and I'm able to achieve my goals more easily.

But it wasn't always easy. For a long time, I wasn't getting results from my meditation and mental rehearsal practice. I was frustrated and gave up on it several times. I felt like I was doing something wrong, and I started to doubt myself.

Then, one day, I had a breakthrough. I realized that meditation and mental rehearsal aren't about reaching a destination. They're about the journey itself. It's about the process of becoming more aware of yourself and your thoughts and emotions. It's about learning to let go of the negative and focus on the positive.

When I started to see meditation and mental rehearsal as a journey of self-discovery and empowerment, I started to see results. I became more patient and persistent, and I was able to stick with my practice even when I didn't see immediate results.

I'm still on my journey, but I'm so grateful for the insights and tools that meditation and mental rehearsal have given me. They've helped me to become more confident and resilient, and they've given me a greater sense of peace and well-being.

THE JOURNEY CONTINUES

We are coming to the end of the book, but the transformation journey has no finish line. The tools and interventions I have shared have been transformational in my own journey, and I hope they will be for you too.

When I first started on this journey, I was scared and uncertain. I didn't know if I could really change my life. But I took a leap of faith and started practicing the tools and interventions. And slowly but surely, I started to see results. I overcame my fears, achieved my goals, and started to live a more fulfilling life.

I encourage you to carve out at least two hours every month to go through the Master Your Inner Game Blueprint. As you complete each tool and intervention, you will find that your dreams will get bigger and new challenges will arise. These tools will help you navigate these challenges and stay clear on what you want.

Remember, mastering your Inner Game is an ultra-marathon, not a marathon. It requires persistence, grit, and endurance. The journey will have its ups and downs, but with the tools and interventions you have learned, you will be better equipped to handle whatever comes your way.

You have the power to transform your life, one step at a time. With every stride, you are getting closer to becoming an even better version of yourself.

Never, ever, ever give up.

Keep going.

I believe in you. You can do this!

Bring it on!

CONCLUSION

Advice to My Younger Self

Embracing Imperfections and
Trusting the Journey

Hey there, younger me.

Take a moment to pause, because I have some words of wisdom
to share.

If I could hop into a time machine and have a heart-to-heart with
you, here's what I would say:

First and foremost, let's talk about the power of a calm mind.

Life is a wild ride, full of unexpected twists and turns.

When the storms hit and the waves threaten to overwhelm you,
remember to take a deep breath.

Practice mindfulness, my dear.

Find solace in the present moment and let that peace radiate from within.

It's in those moments of stillness that you'll find the strength to weather any storm.

Now, listen closely: mistakes are not the enemy. In fact, they're your greatest teachers.

You're going to make some colossal mistakes. Embrace them.

Everyone, and I mean everyone, makes mistakes. It's a natural part of this crazy journey called life.

So, embrace those missteps. Learn from them, grow from them, and use them as stepping-stones to something greater.

And please, don't let the weight of your mistakes hold you down.

You are not defined by your failures, but by the resilience and determination with which you rise from them.

Ah, perfection. Let's address this pesky notion head-on. Spoiler alert: It doesn't exist.

Trust me, I've searched high and low for it, and it's about as real as a unicorn riding a rainbow.

Embrace your imperfections, my dear.

They are what make you beautifully human.

Strive for excellence, yes, but don't let the pursuit of an unattainable ideal rob you of the joy and satisfaction found in simply being yourself.

You are enough, just as you are.

Speaking of being yourself, surround yourself with positive souls who lift you higher.

The people you choose to share your journey with have a profound impact on your happiness and growth.

Seek out those who see your potential, who believe in your dreams, and who cheer you on when you need it most.

Distance yourself from those who bring you down or dim your light.

You deserve a tribe that celebrates your authenticity and lifts you up when you falter.

Now, let's get to the heart of the matter.

Belief, my dear, is your secret weapon.

Believe in yourself, even when the world tries to shake your confidence.

Your belief in yourself is a force that can move mountains and defy expectations.

Trust your abilities, your intuition, and your dreams. Nurture that flame of self-belief, for it will guide you through the darkest nights and lead you to the brightest horizons.

Oh, and one more thing: Your mind may think, but your heart knows.

In a world that often overwhelms you with choices and opinions, remember to listen to the whispers of your heart.

Your heart knows your true desires, your passions, and your purpose. Trust its gentle nudges, even when your mind insists on analyzing every decision to death.

Sometimes, my dear, the most courageous and fulfilling paths are the ones that feel right in your heart, even if they defy logic.

So, younger me, take these words to heart. Embrace the imperfections, the mistakes, and the power of belief. Trust the journey, for it has remarkable things in store for you. You are capable of achieving the extraordinary, and I want you to always believe in yourself and your dreams. Now go forth, my dear, and conquer the world with your beautiful, imperfect, and courageous self.

One last thing: Never, ever, ever, ever, ever forget that your family is everything. Make memories with them.

Your biggest believer

MODELS

The Inner Game Spiral

INNER GAME

MASTERING

EMERGING

DOING

THINKING

STEP 1: THINKING

In this book, I have provided you with several interventions on how to go deeper with your thinking, and how to cultivate a deeper sense of future self-awareness.

Being aware of your thoughts, triggers, and automatic responses that you're trying to break is the first step.

For example, if you're someone who meditates for an hour in the morning, great, but what about the rest of the day? Who are you being for the majority of your waking hours? Who are you trying to be?

In this step, we are developing the model of our Future-Self.

These interventions will provide ideas of attributes you aspire to embody.

What are the attributes of your Future-Self?

How do you want to think?

How do you want to talk?

What words do you want to use?

How do you want to feel?

STEP 2: DOING

In this step, we take the model of our Future-Self, and we start making new choices that are aligned with the new state of being we're trying to embody.

It all starts with making new choices! In other words, moving from the known to the unknown.

The known is all about your current choices, the choices of how to think, feel, and act.

The unknown is the realm of new choices, new ways of thinking, feeling and acting.

STEP 3: EMERGING

Having a clear model and embodying it gives the new personality a shape and form. It's no different from athletes or actors watching themselves perform their craft. In those moments, the gap between who they are, and who they are trying to be, starts to emerge.

Emerging is when you go from thinking to doing. You'll notice your personality shifting, and your body is starting to create new chemicals, which will shift your energy.

As your energy shifts, a new personal reality will start to emerge for you.

You are now starting to become that elevated energy!

STEP 4: MASTERING

In this step, you hit the reset button.

Going from limited emotions to elevated emotions.

When we embark on the journey of self-improvement, our bodies may resist the change that we are trying to bring about.

This resistance is because our body is accustomed to its current state and finds comfort in familiarity. However, this resistance is a sign that we are getting closer to making a breakthrough.

It's important to note that this journey of self-improvement is not a linear path. It's a spiral, and we will revisit the same steps many times, with each repetition bringing us closer to our goals.

To those of you who are struggling, I want to congratulate you and welcome you to this journey. You are doing everything right. Every time you fall, get back up and keep going.

Remember that there's no such thing as failure in this work, only opportunities for learning, feedback, and growth.

We can continue to learn, rehearse, and experiment with new ways of thinking and behaving.

By staying committed to this journey and believing in ourselves, we can become the best version of ourselves.

STEP 1: THINKING

Envision a new future for yourself or your organization. What would it be like for you to be less stressed and more creative?

STEP 2: DOING

Identify habitualized patterns that keep you from moving toward that new future on an individual level.

STEP 3: EMERGING

Use the process, models, and tools from the workshop to rewire the brain and unlock the potential of that new, improved future state.

STEP 4: MASTERING

Changed individuals collectively from more engaged teams who are then ready to step into that new future of a transformed organization.

ACKNOWLEDGMENTS

Gratitude and Appreciation: It is with the deepest sincerity that I say I love each one of you, and will forever be grateful to you.

Jasmine Harchandani

Marrying Jasmine has been the best decision I ever made. She is the most loving and supportive person I know. She is always there for me, no matter what. She is my lighthouse in the stormy seas of life, supporting me through the darkest nights and celebrating the brightest moments. She is the best wife I could ever dream of, and the finest mother. I love her more than words can say.

To my children, Arhan and Mikhayl Harchandani

I am so grateful to be the father of such amazing children. You are both smart, funny, and kind. I am so proud of the young men you are becoming.

I know that I am not perfect, and I will make mistakes along the way. But I promise that I will always love you unconditionally and be there for you no matter what.

You are my greatest teachers. You show me the power of love, the importance of laughter, and the beauty of the world. I am so grateful to be your father and to watch you grow and learn.

I know that you will both do great things in life. I believe in you with all my heart.

I love you more than words can say.

My dad, Prakash Harchandani

I wouldn't be the person I am today without my father's influence. He has instilled in me a passion for adventure, travel, and technology.

I remember when I was just a child, he would tell me stories about his adventures in far-off lands. These stories sparked my imagination and fueled my desire to see the world for myself.

He also taught me the importance of curiosity and learning. He was always tinkering with new gadgets and devices, and he encouraged me to do the same. He taught me how to take things apart and put them back together, which helped me to develop a tactile approach to learning. This hands-on learning style has been an asset throughout my journey as an entrepreneur.

I am so grateful for everything he has done for me. He is my role model, and I aspire to be as curious, adventurous, and intelligent as he is.

My mom, Chandra Harchandani

My mother has always been my rock. She has been there for me through thick and thin, and she has always been my biggest supporter.

She has taught me the importance of humility, gratitude, and positivity. She has shown me how to be strong and independent, and she has always encouraged me to follow my dreams.

I am so grateful for everything my mother has done for me. She is my role model, and I aspire to be as kind, compassionate, and strong as she is.

Guddie Jain

My sister, Guddie, is my best friend. She is always there for me, no matter what. She is the happiest and most grounded person I know, and she always knows how to make me laugh.

I remember when I was going through a difficult time in my life. I was feeling lost and alone, but Guddie was always there for me. She listened to me without judgment and offered me wise counsel. She helped me to stay grounded and to find the joy in life again.

Guddie is the most kind and compassionate person I know. She is always willing to help others, and she always puts others before herself. She is a role model for me, and I aspire to be as kind and compassionate as she is.

Bharti Badlani

My mother-in-law is one of the strongest people I know. She has faced many challenges in her life, but she has always come out stronger. She is a survivor and an inspiration to me.

The Harchandani, Jain, Bhojwani and Badlani Family

I am so grateful to each and every one of you. You are my family, and I am so proud and blessed to be able to call you that.

I am grateful for your love and support. I am grateful for your guidance and wisdom. You have taught me so much about life, and I am a better person because of each of you.

I am grateful for your laughter and your tears. You have shared so many memories with me, both happy and sad. I will cherish them forever.

I am grateful for your presence in my life. You make me feel loved and accepted, and I am so lucky to have you.

I love you all very much.

Eben Pagan

Your impact on my life will continue to ripple into my future self as I continue to reinvent myself because of you. You have taught me more about myself than anyone I have ever met.

Thank you kindly, dear friend.

Annie Lala

Thank you for making me believe in a more profound love that has improved all my relationships.

Dr. Linda Wahab

I want to express my heartfelt gratitude for your invaluable support along the way, and in helping me brainstorm the title of my book. Your creative input and thoughtful suggestions played a significant role in shaping the final title, and I couldn't be more thrilled with the result.

Lou

Of the many things you have taught me, the most powerful lesson was that sincerity is all about honesty and authenticity. I salute you.

Anand Rao

Your profound mentorship has helped me expose and break my childhood patterns. Your mastery of energy techniques has been priceless in my journey and coaching practice.

Robert Simic

The very first moment you asked me about my limiting beliefs, to which I replied, "I have none", was the moment you woke me up to the recurring patterns playing out in my life and career. I woke up to the Inner Game when you helped me discover the insidious beliefs that hindered me. Your impact on my life is immeasurable.

Dr. Joe Dispenza

Through your work I have witnessed joy I've never seen. I witnessed an immense amount of gratitude from people. I felt people open their hearts wide. I witnessed people shine for each other. I witnessed people have mystical experiences. It was incredible. I'm eternally grateful to you and your body of work.

Rob Foster

When the topic of big goals comes up, specifically around Ironman, I'm usually asked, "How did you do it?" My coach, Rob Foster, has kept me honest, called me out when he needed to, and elevated me when I worked for it. He held me accountable all the way!

A great coach is hard to find, but when you do, you become better at life.

Inner Fight Community

I've been a part of the Inner Fight Community for over a year now, and it's been incredible. The daily support and banter have been so helpful in keeping me motivated and on track. I've learned so much from the other members, and I've made some great friends.

I'm so grateful to be a part of this community. It's made a huge difference in my life, and I know it will continue to do so for many years to come.

The Inner Fight Community is one of those rare communities that truly uplifts and supports its members. I'm so proud to be a part of it.

Andrea Zoia

I am grateful to my dear friend and coach, Andrea Zoia for her guidance and friendship. She helped me to elevate my confidence and presence and to sharpen my message so that I could connect with a broader audience. It's been a blessing to learn and grow with you.

Sanjay Raghunath

My mentor and friend, Sanjay has taught me how to think critically, creatively, and with humility. He has also shown me the importance of servant leadership. I am so grateful for his mentorship.

VCA, GSA, Genius, NCS, and OPM Masterminds

I am so grateful for the group of people who have allowed me to be vulnerable with them. You have shown me that it is okay to be myself, even when I am not perfect. You have not judged me but have instead offered support and encouragement. You have pushed me outside my comfort zone, helping me to grow and learn. You have let me into your world, sharing your stories and experiences with me. And you have trusted me, with your secrets and your hearts. I am so lucky to have you in my life. You have made me a better person, and I am so grateful for your friendship.

Entrepreneurs Organization

I would like to acknowledge with gratitude an organization of amazing people who have generously enhanced my life with their time, love, and wisdom over the last few years. To everyone that I have served on the board with, and to those I have been in forum with, each of you has left an indelible mark in my life.

Rajeev Daswani and a Happiness Center

Rajeev has inspired me to be more vulnerable and to lead with love and compassion. He has been a true friend and I am grateful for his support.

Rajiv Whabi

Rajiv is a supportive and challenging friend who has helped expand my perspective with his insights. I am grateful for his friendship and guidance.

Dana Alhanbali, Ahmed Al Baker, Lerang Selolwane, Advait Chaturvedi, Akheel Jinabhai, Eric Grenouilleau, Brian Ah-Chuen, Satya Yerramsetti, Dele Nedd, Shilpa Kane, Gautam Aggarwal, Hanan Nagi, Mufaddal Abbas, Fadi Farra, Raju Sennik, Vishal Kirpalani

I want to express my sincere thanks for reading the first draft of my book. Your support and feedback mean the world to me. Your insights have made this journey richer, and I'm grateful for your time and encouragement.

Nikos Acuna

I am so grateful for our 25-year friendship. Nikos has inspired me and challenged me intellectually in so many ways. He has always been willing to have deep and vulnerable conversations with me, and he has never shied away from challenging my beliefs. I am so grateful to him for helping me grow as a person. He has made me a better friend, a better thinker, and a better person. I am so lucky to have him in my life.

Chezard Ameer

I am grateful for Chezard's friendship. He is a true friend who is always honest with me. He challenges me to be the best version of myself, and he always gives me the most objective advice when I need it. I know that I can always count on him, and I appreciate his support more than he knows.

Sucha Bansal

I am so grateful to have him in my life. He is one of my oldest and dearest friends, and I consider him to be a brother. He has been there for me through thick and thin, and I know that I can always count on him.

He is the most loyal and supportive friend anyone could ask for. I am so grateful to have him as my friend. He is a true brother, and I cherish our friendship.

He has helped me to think more critically, and to see the world in a new way.

AUTHOR BIO

*D*hiren Harchandani is a perpetual student of transformation, leadership, and mindset. With over two decades of experience spanning five industries, he has a proven track record of founding and successfully exiting ventures. His dedication to transformational coaching has led him to mentor entrepreneurs, collectively contributing to businesses with total revenue exceeding $3 billion. As a TEDx speaker, he passionately advocates for unlocking human potential.

A graduate of Harvard Business School's OPM program, Dhiren combines strategic acumen with over 2,500 hours of coaching experience to catalyze leaders and organizations, fostering greater engagement, creativity, and productivity. His approach integrates a dynamic blend of NLP, neuroscience, and psychology to achieve transformative results.

Beyond his professional pursuits, Dhiren is an adventure enthusiast, constantly pushing his limits by competing in Ironman races and scaling mountains. His passion for exploration has taken him to more than 70 countries, spanning all seven continents.

Above all, he champions his family life, relishing time with family, and wholeheartedly embracing his affection for dogs.

EXTRAS

THE INNER GAME TEST

If you're an Entrepreneur, this Inner Game Test is for you.

This is one of the most important tests that you will take. I can say that confidently because I've taken all my personal experience, everything I've learned from my coaching practice, from ancient wisdom, and from the school of self-development, to design this test.

It's important to understand how strong your Inner Game is. Not being aware will leave you feeling stuck which may lead to experiencing the same results repeatedly.

This test will take you three minutes to complete, it's made up of ten thought-provoking questions that are simple, yet very powerful, and it will instantly reveal to you your strengths and your opportunities for growth.

Moreover, it will reveal the triggers that have been sabotaging your success and what's been holding you back; this process alone will give you a hard reset.

If you want to Master Your Inner Game and take your business to the next level, you have to take your thinking, your self-image and your self-esteem to the next level as well.

To take the Inner Game test, please visit: www.dhirenharchandani.com

THE INNER GAME CLARITY EXERCISE

How would you like to get more clarity?

This exercise will help you to consciously access parts of your neurology that you haven't visited before. Developed and backed up by decades of language and Quantum Linguistics, this exercise will reveal the effect on our neurology.

To access the Inner Game Clarity Exercise, please visit:

www.dhirenharchandani.com/clarity

CONNECT WITH ME

Dhiren P. Harchandani

Speaker, Executive Coach, Entrepreneur, Endurance Athlete

Inner Game Consulting

Email: transform@dhirenharchandani.com

Website: www.dhirenharchandani.com

Social Media Handles:
LinkedIn: linkedin.com/in/dhirenharchandani

Instagram: instagram.com/dhirenharchandani

Notes

www.ingramcontent.com/pod-product-compliance
Lightning Source LLC
Chambersburg PA
CBHW031846200326
41597CB00012B/297